VOICES FOR

One World is a new group within the Labour
movement to bring Socialist ideas to bear on the problems of poverty-stricken people and countries. For the
past year, we have been making efforts to stimulate
awareness about the real causes of underdevelopment.

We have been pressing the Government to face its
responsibilities towards other nations, instead of cutting
its aid budget.

We have been explaining the links between world
poverty and international business and finance.

We have been co-operating with the voluntary aid
agencies and people from the poor countries in making
the case for practical policies to help our fellow men and
women make a permanent escape from hunger and want.

One World stands for:

PEACE and an end to the arms trade that wastes
billions of pounds and thousands of lives every year.
Three quarters of our arms exports go to the Third World
– much of it equipment for use by repressive regimes
against their own people.

EQUALITY between regions of the world, between
races, and between men and women. Women are the
poorest of the poor. Their contributions as workers,
farmers, carers and teachers are crucial to successful
development. And yet they are taken for granted. They
are the "invisible majority".

DEMOCRACY and the fundamental right of majorities
to decide the future of their country. We oppose the
refusal of the British Government to bring in real sanctions against the racially repressive regime in South
Africa.

FREEDOM from hunger, poverty and oppression. We
condemn the abuse of power by industrial countries –

East and West – by governments, international banks, multinational corporations and commodity and financial markets. None of us would ask an already poor country to choose between providing basic health care and paying back high interest rates to European banks. Nor should our governments.

We believe that the activities of aid agencies and charities to help the people of the poor countries are essential – but can not be enough. To defeat famine and want it is necessary for governments – acting singly and through international organisations like the United Nations – to provide development aid, to cut debt burdens, and to pay fair prices for the produce of the poor countries.

The fact of modern life is that we are all interdependent. There are no boundaries to pollution or disease. Poverty spreads because the poor cannot buy. War wastes the precious resources of the planet as it causes misery and death. The destruction of the environment in any continent affects every continent.

And because these are common dangers they have common answers: co-operation and concerted action.

Ours is a global community, and in One World we work for practical action which will strike at the very roots of poverty and exploitation, the ruin of the natural environment and the terrible waste of money and lives.

Join us as a partner in the struggle against poverty. We are not the leaders but the *sharers* of a common humanity. That is why we make common cause.

Please address any enquiries to: One World, 1 Darenth Road, London, N16 6EP

ALL PROCEEDS FROM THE SALE OF THIS BOOK WILL GO TO ONE WORLD

GLENYS KINNOCK

VOICES FOR ONE WORLD

FONTANA/Collins

First published in 1988 by Fontana Paperbacks
8 Grafton Street, London W1X 3LA

Copyright © One World 1988

Printed and bound in Great Britain by
William Collins Sons & Co. Ltd, Glasgow

CONDITIONS OF SALE

This book is sold subject to the condition that
it shall not, by way of trade or otherwise, be
lent, re-sold, hired out or otherwise circulated
without the publisher's prior consent in any
form of binding or cover other than that
in which it is published and without a similar
condition including this condition being
imposed on the subsequent purchaser.

CONTENTS

Introduction

GLENYS KINNOCK

The daughter of a railway signalman, Glenys Kinnock comes from Anglesey, North Wales.

She graduated from University College Cardiff, Wales in History and Education and also obtained the Diploma in Education. Mrs Kinnock is currently teaching at the Wykeham Junior and Infants School in North London, where she specialises in reading development. She has a particular interest in multi-cultural education.

Mrs Kinnock has had a lifelong involvement in the Labour Party, the women's movement, the Campaign for Nuclear Disarmament and the Anti-Apartheid Movement. She has also written widely in the British press on education, the health service and development issues.

In May 1986 Mrs Kinnock, with several leaders of the Labour and Trade Union Movement, launched the One World campaign. The purpose of the group is to increase public support and understanding in Britain, especially in the Labour Movement, for a change in North/South trade and relations and in the direction and use of development support.

Glenys Kinnock is forty-three years old. She married Neil Kinnock in 1967, and they have two children, Stephen and Rachel. They live in London.

The Ethiopian famine of 1985 was unique. Not in its misery nor its devastation nor its despair. In all of those it was tragically typical of so many times and so many countries. What was extraordinary about that disaster was the way it was conveyed to the people of the industrialised countries. Television journalists who were clearly shaken by what they saw wanted the world to shake itself too. With undisguised purpose, they broadcast the famine with passion and compassion.

The result was a series of activities that had never been seen before. Rock stars and other leading figures in popular culture mobilised themselves to raise enough money through "Live Aid" and its myriad successors. It was a great testimony of humanity. And apart from the way in which it helped to relieve suffering, it also gave new encouragement to those who for years had been trying to stimulate understanding and positive responses to the suffering and insecurity of the world's poor.

In Britain, where the general public's readiness to give was enthralling, a group of people in the Labour movement – all of them with a long-term commitment to various aid charities – got together to consider how this fresh consciousness could be built upon. We wanted it to be informed so that it could help to achieve the longer-term objectives of securing change in political and economic policies and in relationships between the rich and the poor parts of the world.

That was when we formed One World. "Live Aid

rocked the world," we said, "but it couldn't roll away the root causes of hunger and poverty. Only effective and continual action by our government and the governments of other industrial countries can do that." So we still work with the charities and we think that every new Band Aid, Sports Aid, Comic Aid, Council Aid initiative and the people who get them going deserve full support.

But – together with churches and charities and trade unions and anyone else who will make the effort – we also keep up the flow of information and go on making the arguments for change. That is where *Voices for One World* comes from. It is a collection of the thoughts, ideas and experiences of people who approach the common questions of development from a wide variety of origins. Some are more participants than observers – individuals who work in the developing world and who have first-hand knowledge of what can and what needs to be done. Others are writing from the North of our world, but from a perspective which recognises that in the final analysis poverty and famine begin here in our hemisphere. All make a clear call for a significant movement of wealth from rich to poor in the interests of the whole world, for aid programmes which ask what people want, for partnership with oppressed minorities and majorities in the Third World. The voices which speak out in this book are all calling for solidarity between human beings.

Of all human beings, children are, of course, the most precious and most vulnerable. They are also the most innocent. And yet a quarter of a million of them die each week from poverty and poverty-related causes in a world that can feed them and save them from disease. We have a responsibility to them to make the world safe, to clear away the menace of nuclear conflict and, as Michael Manley tells us, to secure a real peace where there are no regional wars to bring death and misery.

A thread which runs through all the chapters of *Voices*

for One World is a recognition of our mutual ability to affect and change each other's lives.

As this book has been prepared, many of its contributors have faced crisis and danger. A high number of them live in areas of conflict where they and their compatriots are being denied rights, respect, self-determination and the chance to achieve self-sufficiency. And, as if these afflictions were not enough, there have been droughts and floods and, of course, depressed commodity prices and crushing debts to face: a catalogue of problems and challenges that seem insurmountable until it becomes clear that the defiance and determination which such people show in the face of adversity creates an unceasing counter-attack against these man-made and natural crises. And then it becomes equally clear that, with some support, they can overcome them.

Their vision of change is more than a dream of a different and better world. It involves a rejection of the morbid idea that poverty, starvation and exploitation will always be with us. It offers rational alternatives to those conditions. Their vision is a perception, illuminated by idealism, expressed with courage. But driven by practicality. These qualities give authority to the people who offer us their knowledge about warfare, pollution, racism, sexism, environmental degradation and a multitude of other issues.

These issues are not new. But they are more awful in effect and demanding more than ever before to be defeated. The problems and challenges are common. They have to be faced with common solutions and common action and with a relationship which is based on mutual growth and respect.

Every time we switch on the television or open a newspaper we are reminded of the interdependence of our world. The explosion at Chernobyl and the radioactive emissions which came from it and spread across half a continent tell us that our technological capability – and sometimes our technical arrogance – have implications for all of us, wherever we live.

Other dangers – less dramatic, more insidious and, cumulatively, equally lethal – threaten life and the means of life. Acid rain in the industrialised countries; rapacious exploitation of land and minerals by commercial interests; and over-farming by the desperate poor in developing countries all poison and punish the earth.

Conflicts in the Middle East, South-East Asia, Southern Africa and Central America are just some of the warnings that the world is living on a hair trigger.

Technological advances have been truly remarkable but this has not meant a commensurate willingess to abandon dominance and the potential for exploitation. The old order carries on claiming new victims. There are more hungry, illiterate and homeless people than there were forty years ago and every two weeks more people die of hunger than died at Hiroshima and Nagasaki. The economic and social dominance of North over South rolls on almost unchecked.

There is obviously a lot to learn about how to tackle the causes of these world problems, and part of the learning process, of course, involves the destruction of myths. The world *does* produce more than enough food to meet the needs of every woman, man and child. Global food production *has* risen faster than the population in the last forty years. Poverty is *not* "caused" by over-population, by weather conditions or by inadequate food resources. There *are* mountains of cereal and over-produced foods in Europe and America. It *is* maldistribution and not scarcity which causes hunger. As the Brandt Report said in 1980, "Mankind has never before had such ample technical and financial resources for coping with hunger and poverty. The immense tasks can be tackled once the collective will is mobilised."

The task of mobilising that "collective will" is formidable but not impossible. The world has common crises. It needs a new programme for co-operation and recovery and that requires a co-ordinated initiative and a focus for all the ordinary people who have dug deep in their pockets and in so doing told the rest of the world, "We want change".

Trade unions are among the agencies that can most obviously develop that focus. They are already, of course, concerned with workers' rights and solidarity around the world. As multinationals spread their net further, trade unions themselves need to become "multinational". As international finance markets send prices soaring and dipping in seconds and ownership alters in hours, trade unions need fast communications and flexible responses.

Carl Wright, with his background of experience at home and abroad, ably discusses the trade unions' relationships with the rest of the world. There is great scope for wider international co-operation, information exchange, joint campaigns and assistance for trade unions in developing countries. Just as trade unions had to organise to cover the whole country in the last century, so trade unions have to build alliances to cover the whole world in this century. And, as always, they are best able to achieve the objectives of solidarity when they combine defence of standards with progressive activities to raise the quality of life of whole societies inside and outside the ranks of trade unionism.

One of the strongest threads winding through the contributions in this book is the recognition that women are everywhere in the frontline of the struggle for advance. The case is clearly made by Ela Bhatt and others for ensuring that women's expertise and inventiveness are properly used and their obligations fully recognised. They are the invisible majority, described in War on Want's "Women for Change" campaign as "everywhere facing discrimination in male-dominated societies".

Poor women in the developing world face a triple struggle: as citizens of underdeveloped countries, as poor people living in the poorest parts of those countries, and as women. What is absolutely incontravertible is that until they gain power for themselves as workers, teachers, managers, and community leaders there will never be substantial progress or change.

That was the compelling message of the UN Decade for Women Conference that met in Nairobi in 1985. The advancement of women and their struggle for their own emancipation and development is an essential part of the struggle for justice and peace. With an immense workload – two-thirds of the world's working hours are done by women – they also have to care for families and homes and cope with the pressures of frequent pregnancies, childbirth and child rearing. Joan Lestor gives us insight into the role of women as carers and teachers and draws attention to the fact that women must be properly recognised as the irreplaceable means of protecting the children of the developing world from ill health and disease. As the UN State of the World's Women report said, "The challenge is to work for women's integration and active participation in development and as beneficiaries and contributors at all levels and to win them justice and equal rights. Because such efforts will benefit not only women but the whole human family they will help secure a better world for us all."

One of the major determinants of the means of creating a fairer world is, as Miguel d'Escoto argues, the attitude to debt. In Latin America 150 million people live in absolute poverty and struggle to cope with the effects of the "structural arrangements" their governments are forced to make. The result of these and other repayment regimes operated in all of the southern continents is that an enormous transfer of wealth from poor debtor countries to Western banks and governments is taking place.

This means that whilst British people were raising funds for aid to the Horn of Africa in 1985, British banks were taking over £1 billion more from countries in the developing world than they were giving them. These countries are coming to resemble a chronically sick person sent on a marathon as a cure. It is becoming clear that the monetarist economics which simultaneously squeeze the poor so that they cannot buy and the people of the industrialised countries so that they cannot sell are what Peru's Democratic Socialist President, Alan Garcia, calls "a philosophy of non production".

The economic instability resulting from debt and depression is contagious. It is clearer now than ever before that for moral and material reasons it is necessary that debts are lifted and rescheduled, that fair commodity prices are paid, usefulness takes the place of usury, and that developing and developed countries have a common advantage to gain in securing a New International Order to plan and promote trade and production and employment in place of the pawn-shop economics of monetarism. Part of that New International Order must be a determination amongst developed countries to provide, and amongst developing countries to seek the means of life rather than the means of death.

Global military spending is hitting the trillion dollar mark at a time, as Joan Ruddock and Michael Manley point out, when all over the world all that people want is peace. Millions are condemned to misery and early death because of the prodigal levels of military expenditure and whatever enemies are shot at, whatever powers are sold to, it is the poor who are the losers in the killing fields.

They are the losers too in the pillage of nature. Gro Harlem Brundtland, who presided over the World Commission on the Environment and Development, highlights in direct fashion that our world is neglecting its natural systems and that there is a growing environmental crisis.

To see hungry people farming eroded soil in a landscape stripped of trees is to know that it is poverty that is causing farmers to destroy the natural environment on which they depend. When people are forced into reliance on cash crops such as coffee, cotton and sugar for their livelihood, none can afford to plant trees, dig wells and build terraces. And when prices for those commodities are cut at the behest of buyers, farming communities and whole countries are made bare and bankrupt.

In India and in East Africa with the awful visual aid of barren soil before my eyes, I learned from many local development workers that development without concern for the environment can only be a short-term, often self-destructive, development. The environment, as the Indian Centre for Science and Environment puts it, is "not just a matter of pretty trees and tigers, threatened plants and ecosystems", it is a matter of eating or not eating, living or not living.

Eating or not eating, living or not living. That is the basic challenge, the elementary cause of the contest against want.

In some places, the battle must be joined because poverty is self-perpetuating, and the inheritance of disadvantage must be halted by education, agricultural and industrial aid and the primary support that will help people to help themselves; in some places there is a need to lift burdens of debt and exploitation so that people can produce and sell without being bowed down by either repayments or ruthlessness; in other places, political and economic liberation and the removal of the costs and injustices inflicted by criminals, imperial powers, terrorists and tyrants are essential to advance as the voices from Latin America, Nicaragua, Kampuchea, the frontline states of Southern Africa and apartheid South Africa itself constantly and convincingly tell us.

Institutions and ideologies continue to conspire to perpetuate the disparities between rich and poor. One World is a movement for peace and justice based in a country with a government which at best ignores and at worst penalises the needy millions. Its policies are not fitted to the realities of the modern world, to British obligations in that world, or to the interests of the British people in a world where we are linked together by bonds of shared humanity and partnership. Because of that its policies will not prevail.

In the 1930s R. H. Tawney wrote:

> Civilization has two aspects. It requires, on the one hand, the conquest by man of his natural environment. It demands, on the other, a habit of discrimination between the relative values of different activities, without which victories are more disastrous than defeats. Half a century ago it could still be assumed that the army was advancing on both fronts and that, in proportion, as the problem of controlling nature was solved, political systems and social institutions would rise to new heights. That creed had its virtues, but facts have been too strong for it . . . It is possible, we now know, for a society to be heir to the knowledge of all the ages and to use it with the recklessness of a madman and the ferocity of a savage . . . Our age is not the first to have reaped the ruin resulting from an enlargement of human powers, unaccompanied by a growth in the capacity to control them. This is the divorce between knowledge and political intelligence.

In Tawney's time – simpler in many ways than ours – that "divorce" brought slump and poverty, the corrupting of science, the enslavement and murder of millions, the triumph of violence as a system of government and prejudice as a system of rule that was only made temporary by world war. Such a discrepancy between "knowledge and political intelligence", between the means of advance and the needs for answers, afflicts the world still.

But because we are, more than ever, part of One World, bound together by common threats and common opportunities, we have common cause to end that divergence.

As the contributors to *Voices for One World* and so many others show, we have the people to do it. We have the potential to do it. We certainly have the reason to do it. All we have to do is to ensure we have the realism to do it.

Glenys Kinnock
South Wales
Easter 1988

Sustainable Development

(Speech at the Nordic Conference on Environment and Development, 1987, Stockholm)

GRO BRUNDTLAND

Born in 1939, Gro Harlem Brundtland graduated from the Medical School of the University of Oslo in 1963 and took a master's degree in public health at Harvard University in 1965. She then worked in medicine until 1974 when her political career took over and she became Minister of the Environment. This post she held until October 1979, when she assumed her seat in Parliament.

In February 1981 she became prime minister, an office which she held until the general election in October of the same year. In April 1981 she took over as leader of the Labour Party, after having served as its deputy leader since 1975.

From October 1981 she was leader of the Labour Party's Parliamentary Group until she resumed her title of prime minister in May 1986.

Gro Harlem Brundtland is Vice President of the Socialist International and a member of the Independent Commission on Disarmament and Security., She is Chairperson of the World Commission on Environment and Development.

Gro Harlem Brundtland is married and has four children.

Who would have thought a quarter of a century ago that environment and development would stand out clearly as the major challenge facing mankind today, when we have only half as many years left to the turn of the millennium? In the early sixties our view of development was so much simpler. Indeed, it was unconditionally optimistic. And – seemingly – with good reason. Our material well-being was improving at a rapid rate. Health was improving all over the world. Peoples who had endured centuries of domination were gaining self-confidence, establishing their own identities as free and sovereign nations. Man's belief in his own power reached a new peak as he penetrated outer space. Growth rates were soaring.

But during these past twenty-five years we have witnessed an ever-increasing body of evidence showing that development has not been only beneficial. We have become increasingly aware that human activity has been systematically destroying important life-support systems. We have certainly been on a fast track, but not on the *right* track.

The Stockholm Conference on the Human Environment in 1972 was the result of growing concern among an informed public who made a political cry for action. And the Stockholm Conference was only the first in a series of international conferences which have been held in response to the frustration among people and nations. The United Nations' Environment Programme emerged from a strong sense of urgency. The conferences on water supply, food, women, human settlements, new and renewable energy sources, those involving people's access to the means to choose the size of their family, all offered a hope of improved co-operation on major issues. Yet a sense of frustration and inadequacy prevailed. The world was growing closer, but the gaps between us were widening.

The World Commission on Environment and Development was established by the General Assembly of the United Nations in 1983. The call from the General Assembly was an urgent one and the Commission's broad mandate reached around the globe. When the Secretary General asked me to establish and lead the Commission, I was afraid that the task set for us was perhaps *too* ambitious.

We were asked to re-examine the critical environment and development problems of the planet and to formulate realistic proposals to solve them. Commissioners from twenty-one countries initiated a series of thorough investigations on all continents, including the broad participation of people through our public hearings. Our findings were indeed mixed. We found success, we found failure and we found a range of in-betweens.

The success stories are many. Infant mortality is declining, human life-expectancy is increasing, the relative number of adults who can read and write is growing, so is the number of children starting school. Global food production is increasing faster than the population is growing. Isolated achievements of momentous importance such as the green revolution and the eradication of small-pox reconfirm our faith in mankind. And our capacity to deal with the first generation of pollution problems is improving although only a few countries have so far succeeded in controlling pollution, and even the rich industrialised countries have not managed to deal with the backlog.

But in dealing with the new generation of environmental issues, all countries are falling behind. Many of the new threats are regional and even global in scale and many raise crucial questions of national security and planetary survival.

In spite of immense progress in many regions, 700 million people are still living in poverty and their numbers are growing every year. Reliable United Nations predictions leave no doubt that many of the least developed countries have experienced serious economic setbacks in recent years. The per capita income in many of them has not been so low since the sixties. Many countries are caught in a vicious circle of economic decline, increasing poverty and environmental degradation.

Falling commodity prices, debilitating burdens of debt, high interest rates, declining financial flows and reductions in aid all add up. They have forced developing countries to overtax their environment in order to pay for imports and accommodate creditors. The gap between North and South is growing. In trying to keep up, the poor countries have no alternative but to produce more raw materials and agricultural goods for export. The system forces them to deplete their mines, and we call it "income". It forces them to harvest twice a year in areas where the soil can hardly sustain *one* harvest. They clear the forests to cultivate new land often ill suited for agriculture. They cut down forests to sell the timber. All this is called "income". And surpluses on the world market press prices down, leaving these countries little option but to apply more of the same medicine. Poverty is both a cause and effect of environmental degradation.

Population growth is inextricably linked to environment and development issues and our success in the fight against poverty will largely determine our success in stabilising the world's population some time during the next century. This year it is estimated that the global population will exceed 5 billion. Close to 100 million people will be added to the world every year.

Ninety percent of this growth will take place in developing countries. The demands for education, health, housing, access to food and energy – especially by the poorest of the poor in rural areas where population growth rates continue to increase – represent enormous challenges. While demand in the rural areas will continue to increase, we can expect millions of poor people to move to the cities, to a life they believe will entail opportunities to leave poverty and misery behind.

But what they leave behind often consists of remnants of once arable land which is now threatened by desertification. That threat is more than real. Forests the size of Denmark are lost every twelve weeks; every nine months an area the size of Switzerland is turned into desert; and world-wide soil erosion is now considered to be Problem No. 1 by the Food and Agricultural Organization.

If we continue to burn fossil fuels at present rates we can be almost certain that at least the world's *oil* reserves will be used up during the coming century. The combustion itself releases carbon dioxide into the atmosphere. The resulting greenhouse effect threatens to gradually warm up the globe as solar heat is trapped near the surface of the earth. Global climatic changes could well be the outcome, entailing dramatic implications for food production and settlement. There is scientific evidence which indicates that a global warm-up would raise the level of the sea enough to flood many low-lying coastal cities and river deltas.

Acidification, which is too well known to us in this part of the world, is becoming a global problem. Other industrial gases threaten the protective ozone shield, and we know no method that can restore it. We face the possibility of its depletion, which could result in an increase in the incidence of cancer and in the extinction of life forms at the base of the marine food chain.

6

All these phenomena stand out as solid evidence of serious mismanagement of vital global issues. They make it absolutely imperative for us to choose a new and better course for the future.

Faced with the facts, one could perhaps expect that the Report of our Commission would paint a gloomy picture; that we would see no way out; that we would join the ranks of the pessimists who have the current evidence and trends on their side – but we didn't. Instead, we found ground for hope. We became convinced that people can co-operate to create a future that is more prosperous, more just and more secure. But for this to happen we must tap human resources and ingenuity and we must design new approaches to managing environmental resources and to sustaining human development.

Two weeks ago when I presented our report to the Secretary General of the United Nations, he said that the name itself, "Our Common Future", represented a challenge to him and to the United Nations. Yes, it is meant as a challenge. But it also imposes an obligation.

"Our Common Future" is not a detailed, final blueprint. It is not a scientific report, although it benefited from having the latest scientific evidence available to the Commission. Nor is it another book about environment and development. Instead it is the result of a broad political process of analysis, learning and debate. It is a unanimous report. Above all it is a political document. The Commission included a Soviet academy member, an American republican, a Chinese professor, a former revolutionary who is now Minister of Finance and Planning of Zimbabwe, a Colombian environmentalist, the Secretary General of the Commonwealth of Nations, an Indonesian Minister of Population, to mention just a few of the members and to indicate some of the variety of background and experience. Nevertheless, we all managed to arrive at a common analysis of the means by which policies can and must be changed to match present and future realities. Our consensus report shows that it is possible to work together for common goals, to find solutions that go beyond national confines and redefine what many regard to be self-interest.

As you know, the overriding political concept upon which our report is founded is that of *sustainable development*. We define sustainable development most simply as paths of progress which meet the needs and aspirations of the present generation without compromising the ability of future generations to meet their needs.

Contrary to widely held beliefs, sustainable development does not imply absolute limits to growth, though it clearly recognises that we are approaching critical thresholds in many areas imposed by the patterns of technology and social organisation. Nor is it a new name for environmental protection. Sustainable development is a concept for economic growth. It reaches far beyond the mandated area of any single international organisation, with the possible exception of the United Nations itself.

Sustainable development does not imply a fixed state. It is a process of change in which economic and fiscal policies, trade and foreign policies, energy, agricultural, industrial and other sectoral policies all aim to induce development paths that are economically, socially and ecologically sustainable. It requires more equitable distribution and equal opportunities within and among nations. It must be a goal for all nations, developed and developing alike. Indeed, it is a goal for the global community as a whole.

But sustainable development cannot, and will not, be achieved in a world ridden by poverty. Our Commission has therefore called for a new era of economic growth, one that is forceful, global and at the same time environmentally sustainable, with a content that enhances the resource base rather than degrading it. We are deeply convinced, as Sonny Ramphal so eloquently illustrated yesterday, that worldwide growth is the only remedy for overcoming mass poverty. But we are equally convinced that sustainable growth can create the capacity to solve environmental problems. The process of economic development must be soundly based on the realities of the stock of capital that sustains it. The environment must become an ally, not a victim of development.

To pursue a new era and quality of growth we need to breathe new life and foresight into international economic relations, which, beset by a variety of problems, work against the interests and opportunities of the developing countries in so many ways. The challenge to the future lies partly in the complex web of national policies, both in rich and in poor countries. And it lies not least in some genuine dilemmas we face when trying to attack the problems. For example, as industrialised countries use fewer materials and less energy in their production, they provide smaller markets for commodities and minerals from the developing countries. Yet, if developing nations focus their efforts upon eliminating poverty and meeting essential human needs, then the domestic demand will increase for agricultural products, manufactured goods and services. The very logic of sustainable development requires internal stimulus to Third World growth.

On the global level, growth is being stifled by heavy debt burdens, depressed commodity prices, protectionism in many industrialised countries and stagnating flows of development finance. Certain short-term positive developments have been offset not least by a considerable worsening of terms of trade. Real commodity prices have not been as low since the international economic depression in the 1930s. The countries of Africa that are almost entirely dependent on one or two commodities for export revenues are drawing especially heavily on non-renewable resources in order to obtain the trade surplus needed to service their debts.

We in the industrialised countries will have to accept

the obligation that international economic relations help rather than hinder the possibility of ecologically sound development. This is our duty. But it is also in our own self-interest.

Many of today's trading patterns also contain a massive transfer of environmental costs from the industrialised world to developing countries. A large part of the most environmentally damaging production processes today takes place in developing countries, where they are not subjected to the stricter environmental requirements of many industrialised countries. The realities of this are that in the difficult trade-off between the need for foreign currency in the short term, and longer-term sound environmental policies, many developing countries feel compelled to sacrifice the environment to gain comparative advantage in international trade. This can also be seen as a subsidy from developing countries to the industrialised world. The pollution cost thus absorbed by developing exporters amounted to approximately US $ 14 billion in 1980 alone. By comparison, total annual developing assistance flowing in the other direction amounts to about US $ 35 billion.

These trends will have to be reversed. Commodity prices must be influenced in order to provide a fair international distribution of income. Official development assistance will have to be improved, both in quantity and quality. Increased capital transfers are absolutely necessary and the transfers must take place in ways that are sensitive to the environment.

Thus sustainability criteria should be an integral part of financial support. Policies will have to be changed accordingly, both nationally and internationally, to realise our full potential for a new era of economic growth. Increased co-operation among developing countries also entails opportunity for economic and social progress and has a great potential that needs to be further explored. The new Commission on South-South co-operation which is being established by Julius Nyerere offers promise for this important dimension of international co-operation.

Clearly, sustainable development also requires that we attain a balance between the population and the carrying capacity of our planet. Only in a world that is safer, one which gives the poor more self-respect and hope for their lives and future, will poor people have real choices, including the choice to limit the size of their families.

Fortunately, discussions of these issues are becoming more nuanced and comprehensive. During the Commission's public hearings in Harare, the Economic Commission for Africa stressed that demographic factors will constitute a daunting challenge in the years ahead as the race between population and economic growth intensifies. There is an *urgent* need for far-reaching population policies to be vigorously implemented by African governments.

Population is not a question of numbers alone. Population policies clearly need to comprise education and health policies too, if we are to realise the potential of future generations. Education for all, especially for women, and family planning services are an absolute must for people to exercise their rights to choose to limit the size of their families.

The production of enough food to feed a doubled world population seems within our reach. But securing access to food for those who need it, and ensuring environmentally sustainable agricultural practices, will require fundamental policy changes. The Commission calls for a shift in global agricultural production patterns. Northern agricultural production systems often run on the basis of large-scale and short-sighted subsidies – and on the intensive use of fertilisers and pesticides. They over-exploit farmland and introduce harmful chemicals into food and water. The rich industrial countries need to examine very carefully the impact of their agricultural surpluses. The practice of dumping surpluses must be halted. At present, these surpluses often go to developing countries in ways that depress prices for local farmers, marginalise the poor, undermine agriculture and suppress the political reform which is so desperately needed.

We call for a reorientation of these policies – to secure farm income, while enhancing rather than undermining the resource base. Much greater resources are needed to promote sustainable agriculture in the Third World, using techniques adapted to local conditions. Western-style ploughing has been a major cause of soil erosion in many areas. Furthermore, overgrazing, land clearance, commercial logging, and slash-and-burn agriculture rob soil of its cover and reduce agricultural yields. We call for a shift of the centres of food production to where the demand is, in Third World countries, and to promote this, we call for a change in the terms of trade in agricultural products.

The threat to the diversity of living species – the genetic resource base – is as closely linked to unsustainable agricultural practices as it is to industrial practices and energy use. Today scientists believe that living species are becoming extinct at alarming rates. On average, nature's own extinction rate is estimated at one species a year. Due to the activity of man the present rates are a hundred times higher, and the species that we endanger are those which have been least documented.

The genetic material in wild species contributes billions of dollars yearly to the world economy in the form of improved crops, new drugs and medicines, and raw material for industry. We cannot afford to continue losing these resources that cannot possibly be restored. We commend the UNEP and other organisations for their untiring efforts to promote the conservation of species and ecosystems, but the collective endeavours are tiny given the magnitude and implications of the problem. The Commission calls for a broad spectrum of measures at all levels, local, governmental, regional and global. We call for sanctuaries to be established, inventories to be kept, agreements to be worked out, including the investigation of a global species convention supported by financial arrangements. Failure will limit options for the future.

Energy supply and use are decisive for economic development, for the environment and for the fight against poverty. The differences in energy consumption between North and South are vast. On average, a person in the industrialised world uses eighty times as much energy as a person in southern Africa. More than half of the world's population relies on fuelwood for cooking, light and heat.

A safe, environmentally sound and economically viable energy programme that will sustain human progress into the distant future is clearly called for. And it is possible, but new dimensions of political will and international co-operation will be required to achieve it.

Developing countries will need much more energy to continue to develop, but we in the North should strive to stabilise our energy consumption. A low energy future is our only viable option. This need not mean shortages. We in the industrialised countries could reduce energy input by 50% and still obtain the same benefits. This would be possible if nations were to make energy efficiency the cutting edge of their energy policies.

A rational approach to energy pricing would promote this. Very rarely do energy prices reflect the cost of damage to health, property and the environment connected with energy consumption. If the recent momentum of energy efficiency is to be maintained, governments will have to designate it as their explicit goal. Oil prices are crucial also for energy efficiency. In order to ensure necessary investments in energy conservation and in the development of alternative sources of energy there is a strong need to stabilise the oil prices at a reasonable level. We recommend that new mechanisms for encouraging dialogue between consumers and producers be explored.

Energy efficiency is not, however, the final solution. No single combination of energy sources that could be sustained into the future exists today. In its search for the policies of tomorrow, the Commission devoted much time to the unresolved problems of nuclear energy. I believe that our discussions of this issue stand out as an example of how minds met as we worked our way through the realities of the arguments. We concluded that the generation of nuclear power is only justifiable if there are solid solutions to the presently unsolved problems to which it gives rise.

Consequently, renewable sources not yet available or developed will have to play a dominant role. Far more funds must be allocated to research in new and renewable sources of energy. If we are to succeed in providing energy for a global population of 10 billion people, broad international co-operation is needed to direct, guide and fund the large-scale research necessary.

I have endeavoured to highlight some of the priorities described in "Our Common Future". The task which the Commission set out to accomplish was to make an analysis of the issues and recommend actions about what needs to be done to change the present clearly unsustainable trends and policies. One of the greatest barriers to change is the organisation of society on the national as well as the international level.

Our analysis is clear. Environment is not a separate sector, distinct from key economic sectors such as industry, agriculture and energy. Environmental agencies need to be upgraded politically and expanded financially, yes, but the real changes will only come about when central economic agencies, such as ministries of finance, energy and others, are held responsible for the environmental effects of their policies.

This implies that economy and ecology will have to merge. Environmental concerns must become an integral part of decision-making at all levels. Sustainable devel-

opment must become the overriding goal of all governments – also in their external relations. Development-
assistance agencies which manage and direct four fifths
of the total Overseas Development Administration must
reorient their policies and ensure that all projects support
sustainable development.

Our report can, and I hope will, serve as a new motivation for a global transition to sustainable development.
But success in achieving this transition will require
increased political will and heightened public pressure to
hold governments and institutions responsible.

The Norwegian Government has now requested all
ministries to review and study the Commission's report
and to compare our domestic and foreign policies against
its principles and recommendations. They have been
asked to note where our present policies differ, and if
they do, to consider what steps can be taken to bring
them into line with the report's recommendations. This
process will be guided by a Board of State Secretaries and
will be taking advice from a broad national hearing
soliciting the views of trade unions, industry, farmers'
associations, fishermen, municipal authorities and private organisations, etc. A broad information campaign is
already under way seeking to inspire a nationwide discussion of the report and its implications. A concrete
example of national political steps that need to be stimu-
lated was yesterday's decision to propose to Parliament
an import duty reduction for cars which satisfy the strict
US exhaust gas requirements.

We will pursue "Our Common Future" on a broad
international basis. We will use it actively to influence
the policies of international organisations. The coming
months will provide ample opportunity for this. The
meetings of the UNDP, UNFPA, UNCTAD VII, UNEP's
Governing Council, WHO, ILO, FAO, etc., will be events
this year, where Norway, in concert with other countries,
will promote the concepts and principles contained in

15

"Our Common Future". Recent examples of co-operation, in particular with the other Nordic countries at meetings of the World Bank and the Asian Development Bank, were excellent starting points of a lasting process.

We believe that sustainable development is a goal and obligation that will strengthen the UN and its specialised agencies, and help restore their credibility and status globally. Sustainable development is a major challenge. It should give added impulse to a revival of multilateralism, a crucial issue, after years of isolationism and lack of understanding for our common responsibilities.

In this way Norway has entered into a process of national and international follow-up and implementation, a type of process that we would hope all countries would choose to initiate.

Sustainable development should not require the creation of new international institutions. At the multilateral level, there is considerable institutional capacity available which should be redirected to serve the cause of sustainable development. This will have implications for budgets, mandates, recruitment and programmes of all international organisations, particularly for the UN system and its specialised agencies. The UN itself and its Secretary General should take the lead in this, co-ordinating the process of making the transition to sustainable development. We call for a UN Board on sustainable development under the chairmanship of the Secretary General. We call upon the General Assembly to transform "Our Common Future" into a UN Action Programme for Sustainable Development. We call for a strengthening of UNEP to be the principal source of environmental data, assessment and reporting, and the principal advocate and agent for change and co-operation on critical environmental and natural resource protection issues. But its fund must be increased considerably to allow it to perform such a catalytic role.

The role of multilateral finance institutions is the key to the transition towards sustainable development. The World Bank has taken a positive attitude towards the World Commission and its report, and I have a clear impression of determination to make a fundamental commitment to sustainable development. The World Bank can become the trendsetter for other finance institutions.

It is not only governments or international institutions that face a giant challenge. The call for change should rest on a broad consensus. Scientists, industry, trade unions, teachers, non-governmental organisations (NGOs), all have important roles to play. I would call upon them as I did in London, Washington and Brussels in meetings with the NGO community and the European and international trade union movement, to use "Our Common Future" as a basis upon which to judge their governments' and the international institutional community's efforts and commitment to sustainable development. In this way the report can engage the creativity and energies of millions of committed people in a global effort to begin the process of change that is called for. Humanity has come to a historic crossroad. We have the capacity to change planetary systems, for better or for worse. The interconnected issues of environment and development aptly illustrate the fact that national and political borders will have to be made more transparent. Ecosystems respect no boundaries. We cannot act as if they did.

Environmental issues teach us that we are all simply neighbours, and that our acts and omissions affect everybody. There is time for a new solidarity, and a new ethic. But we must begin now.

The Nordic countries have a special responsibility. We live in a corner of the globe where social tensions are low. We value equality and the just distribution of income.

We are few in number, but our opportunities are many, and our responsibility is great.

Responding to the Crisis: Development NGOs in Britain

KEVIN WATKINS

Kevin Watkins is a freelance journalist, and was formerly
Development Desk Officer for the Catholic Institute for
International Relations.

Introduction

For the majority of developing countries the 1980s, the
United Nations' Third Development Decade, have been
an unmitigated disaster. In many countries real incomes
have fallen to the level of one, or even two, decades ago
and disturbing increases in malnutrition and infant mortality levels have been recorded throughout Latin America, sub-Saharan Africa and Asia. The deepening poverty
behind these grim realities has been rooted not in some
random configuration of economic forces but, to an
important extent, in the structure of North-South
relations.

Recession in the industrialised countries, provoked by
the deflationary economic policies of the early 1980s, has
been transmitted to the South through the mechanisms
of international trade and finance. The most visible result
is the $1.2 trillion Third World debt and unprecedented
outflows of capital which have been associated with it.
With their debt service obligations growing exponentially
and export earnings either static or in decline, many
countries are now technically bankrupt. Constant rounds
of commercial bank rescheduling and continued debt
servicing through deflation have become empty gestures
designed to maintain confidence in an unstable international financial system at the expense of the poorest
nations and most vulnerable people.

It might have been hoped that the depth of the development crisis facing the South would have encouraged a North-South dialogue and prompted the adoption of co-operative international solutions to what are clearly global problems. In fact, the opposite has happened. To an increasing extent the developed countries have used their domination of the Bretton Woods institutions – the World Bank, the International Monetary Fund and the General Agreement on Tariffs and Trade (GATT) – to the detriment of Third World interests. Financial orthodoxies premised upon deflation, devaluation and trade liberalis-ation have been imposed upon developing countries, under the misleading rubric of "structural adjustment", with little reference to human welfare criteria. Moreover, the major multilateral lending agencies and most OECD governments remain wedded to the idea that an acceler-ated recovery in the North constitutes the precondition for recovery in the South. But apart from the fact that the OECD recovery has done little to alleviate the develop-ment crisis to date, with developing countries' terms of trade and debt service ratios continuing to deteriorate, the stockmarket crash of October 1987 has served as a timely reminder of fragile "credit card" foundations.

In the North there has been a growing public awareness of the links between the development crisis in the South and the economic policies of industrialised nations. But this awareness has, in most countries, failed to signifi-cantly influence the political agenda. The spontaneous outbursts of public sympathy which accompany inten-sive media coverage of famines are all too easily dissi-pated when the cameras go elsewhere and life returns to normal. "Normal" in this case, being the ongoing "silent tragedy" of hunger which claims thirty children's lives every minute and condemns 800 million of the world's inhabitants to grinding poverty. It is this underlying human tragedy which places a moral responsibility upon the public in the North to *understand* and *change* the structures of underdevelopment. At a national level, this

22

requires those working in development education to both raise awareness and mobilise support for policy reforms directed towards the restructuring of North-South relations.

Thatcherism and the Neo-Conservative Revolution

For development non-government organisations (NGOs) in Britain, the 1980s have posed immense challenges. Those with overseas programmes and partners have first-hand experience of the human tragedy behind the development crisis. Many, indeed, have been forced to adjust their project work in order to cushion the poor from some of the worst ravages of the debt crisis and structural adjustment. The maintenance of primary health care facilities by NGOs in the face of enforced government retrenchment in welfare spending is a case in point.

Development NGOs have also had to adapt their development education and lobbying work to a changing political environment at home. The election of Margaret Thatcher's Conservative Government in 1979 marked a watershed in post-war political history and, as both her critics and admirers would probably agree, the past eight years have witnessed a transformation of the social and economic face of Britain. In short, the 1980s have been dominated by what has aptly been termed a Neo-Conservative counter-revolution. Along with other bodies in the voluntary sector, development agencies have been forced to confront and respond to its increasingly radical and self-confident agenda.

The hallmark of Neo-Conservatism in Britain has been a profound *laissez faire* ideological assault on the welfare state and the social democratic political and economic consensus upon which it was built. Behind the populist banners of privatisation and "getting government off the back of the people", the message has been unmistakably clear: politics must be subordinated to the presumed dictates of the market and its most sanctified element, the price mechanism.

Admittedly, the ascendancy of Neo-Conservatism has not been without its ironies and outright self-deceptions. In the name of "free-market" popular capitalism, the state has underwritten the sale of public assets to private monopolies at give-away prices; in the name of liberty it has undermined the rights of trade unions and elected local authorities and censored the press by resort to arcane national security legislation; while proclaiming the sovereignty of consumer choice and individualism, it has deprived millions of the right to gainful employment, housing and adequate health-care facilities.

But behind the doublespeak language of free-market capitalism, Thatcherism has held to a consistent political project. In economic policy it has inverted the Keynesian model – which sought to resolve tendencies towards high unemployment and recession by expanding and redistributing demand downwards – by deflation and the redistribution of economic resources upwards. Out of the £19 billion given away in tax cuts between 1979 and 1986 for example, over half went to the richest 10%. The economic rationale behind this redistribution is that tax cuts and state handouts to large corporations constitute the quickest route to an investment-based recovery. In reality, while it has enhanced the incomes of a few and generated a credit and consumer spending boom, it has abjectly failed to promote a sustained recovery in investment levels. At the other end of the spectrum, the abolition of Wage Councils and reduction of social welfare benefits have been used to "price" the unemployed back into the market. The result has been a dramatic increase in the numbers on low wages and a rise in the number of those on or below the poverty line from 6 million to over 9 million since 1979. Where "market forces" have not prevailed, the inherent authoritarianism of monetarist policy has been readily apparent, as when the police were deployed as a paramilitary force against striking miners.

Perhaps the most significant achievement of Thatcherism, however, has been its ability to create a popular base for its social and economic projects through a pervasive free-market ideology. Its creation of a new conventional wisdom and common sense based upon individualism and utilitarianism can no longer be treated as an insignificant or transitory side-effect. Admittedly, Mrs Thatcher herself has contributed little by way of theory to this ethos, but she has created a fertile popular soil for the propagation of the world view of think tanks and research institutes – such as the Institute of Economic Affairs, the Adam Smith Institute, the Centre for Policy Studies and the US-based Heritage Foundation – which in an earlier era would have remained on the lunatic fringes of political life.

Instead of concerning itself with the alleviation of fast rising levels of poverty, the state has actively set about criminalising the poor through changes in the social welfare system and the promotion of media campaigns against "scroungers". Principles of social obligation and the right of individuals to adequate state support in times of need have been displaced by the ethos of charity, the survival of the fittest and outright greed. One side-effect has been a sharp increase in the level of street crime as the poor, imbued with the spirit of Neo-Conservatism but left out of the market-based recovery, pursue non-market forms of income enhancement.

Nine years before her election Mrs Thatcher herself aptly summarised the Neo-Conservative view on social equality as follows: "What is it that impels this powerful and vocal lobby in Britain to press for greater equality. . .often the reason boils down to an undistinguished combination of bourgeois guilt and social envy." It is this reasoning towards equality which continues to guide Conservative thinking today, automatically marginalising groups such as overseas development NGOs and domestic welfare voluntary agencies working to improve the position of the poor.

The Development Agencies Agenda in the 1980s

During the 1970s, development NGOs in Britain generally built their campaigning and educational work around the agenda at the New International Economic Order (NIEO). This was adopted at the sixth United Nations General Assembly and represented a turning point in the dialogue between North and South. The overriding theme of the NIEO was the demand for structural changes in North-South relations. Development models emphasising collective self-reliance and the creation of a more responsive and representative multilateral framework were accepted by the international community as preconditions for sustained recovery. The Integrated Programme for Commodities (IPC) negotiated at the United Nations Conference on Trade and Development (UNCTAD) 4 in 1976, with its focus upon the broad range of problems confronting developing country commodity exporters, represented the zenith of the NIEO era. Its death throes, and most comprehensive popular expression, came in the form of the first *Brandt Report*, which unhappily coincided with the dawning era of monetarism and world recession. The Neo-Conservative assault upon the social democratic consensus, built around Keynesian economics and the welfare state, deprived the *Brandt Report* of a potential political base in Britain. Nonetheless, the *Report* became an important rallying point for NGO activity, with the World Development Movement and other agencies organising a mass lobby of parliament to demand governmental support for its main conclusions.

Against the policy background of the time, it was inevitable that this demand would fall upon stony ground. With the Conservatives committed to slashing public expenditure and freeing market forces at home, there was little prospect of them being guided by the Keynesian-style economic management policies propounded by Brandt abroad. Moreover, in the face of a major assault upon the poor unleashed by the combination of recession and welfare cuts, the plight of the vulnerable in developing countries was never likely to unduly stimulate governmental concern. But the *Brandt Report* also came under criticism from some of the more radical NGOs and independent commentators. In particular, the tendency, which it shared with the World Bank and others, to equate the interests of the Third World poor with those of their national states was attacked as both economistic and utopian.

Whatever differences existed between agencies in their treatment of the *Brandt Report*, its popular appeal underlined the depth of public support for changes in North-South relations. Four years after its publication this became even more apparent as media coverage of the Ethiopian famine sparked off an unprecedented outpouring of spontaneous public compassion. In the course of a little over a year the public more than doubled their level of donations to the major voluntary relief agencies. The horrifying scale of the famine also swelled the ranks of another lobby on Parliament in October 1985, to over 20,000 – the largest for fourteen years. Along with the established charities, new organisations such as Band Aid and Sports Aid sprang up and were swept along by the strength of public feeling. For their part, the agencies were able to channel sympathy into concrete development projects overseas and development education at home. Almost overnight the famine transformed the environment in which development NGOs were operating. After six years of Conservative government, the public itself had demonstrated the limits to the Neo-Conservative individualist ideology by displaying a generosity and compassion which it had failed to curtail.

Although concern over the plight of sub-Saharan Africa has waned, development NGOs have succeeded through their educational work in maintaining the momentum of public concern. Since one of the first acts of the Conservative Government on taking office was the elimination of public spending on development education, this has been a welcome breakthrough.

Broadly speaking there have been three distinctive, though interrelated, styles of educational work. First, major "rolling" campaigns – such as Oxfam's "Hungry for Change" and Cafod's "Proclaim Jubilee" – built upon the involvement of local groups have broadened and deepened the popular base of the development agencies. Second, more focussed campaigning – such as War on Want's "Profits out of Poverty" – has increased public awareness of the role of the British banking system in the international debt crisis. Finally, work with parliament and the mass media has become an increasingly important dimension of NGO work, the purpose being to channel public concern in a politically influential direction.

At the same time as expanding their educational programmes, NGOs have increasingly developed sophisticated analyses of the structural causes of underdevelopment. The economistic focus of the 1970s and early 1980s has given way to a concern to examine the multifaceted character of underdevelopment. This has involved coming to terms with a broad range of economic, social and political issues ranging from debt to disarmament, foods security, ecology and human rights.

28

Aid and Trade

When the Conservative Government came to power in 1979, it had a clear perspective on the future direction of aid policy, namely "to give greater weight in the allocation of our aid to political, industrial and commercial considerations alongside our basic development objectives". In this it has unquestionably succeeded, with a marked reduction in the quality of the aid programme being the most immediate result. To an increasing extent, the Overseas Development Administration has fallen under the influence of the Department of Trade and Industry, where it is seen as a useful export promotion body. Thus the Aid Trade Provision of the aid budget, which is used to enlarge overseas markets for British industry, now accounts for 10% of total aid spending compared to less than 5% eight years ago. While this is good news for corporations such as Balfour Beatty and GEC, the benefits to the Third World poor of the trunk roads and nuclear power stations they provide are more difficult to discern.

In keeping with its free-marketeering ethos, the Conservative Government has also cut the aid budget in quantitative terms. Between 1978/79 and 1985/86 overseas aid fell by some 17% in real terms (more than any other budgetary head except housing), and from 0.5% to 0.3% of gross national product (GNP). Whereas in 1979 Britain was the leading aid donor in the group of seven major industrialised nations, today it is fifth, and as low as twelfth in the overall OECD league. The UN's 0.7% of GNP aid target has become an increasingly distant goal. If the paltry level of US aid (0.24% of GNP) is discounted from the average the British performance is even more discouraging, representing slightly over half the European average for example. It is especially striking to note that Britain was one of only three OECD countries to cut its aid budget in real terms during the first half of the 1980s, with aid to sub-Saharan Africa being cut by as much as 15%. If one of the moral measures of a government and society is its readiness to support those in need, the Conservatives have performed badly abroad as well as at home.

This was especially apparent in the response to the Ethiopian famine when the British Government set new standards in tight-fistedness by transferring emergency relief expenditure from the (much reduced) existing aid budget rather than making new resources available. An all-party Select Committee set up to report on the famine, in a masterly exercise of understatement, concluded that "the generosity of the British people had not been matched by the British Government". Even more disconcerting was the report, in October 1985, of the all-party group on overseas development. This noted a decline of one third in the value of UK agricultural aid to sub-Saharan Africa and a negligible level of spending on subsistence rain-fed agriculture. The bulk of British aid to African agriculture remains concentrated on the large-scale production of export crops, especially in those areas where British multinationals have a major commercial interest.

Unsurprisingly, development NGOs have fought a defensive struggle to maintain the aid budget, but they have also demanded an improvement in its quality. There is now a consensus that the Aid Trade Provision should be heavily cut back or removed altogether. Beyond this there is concern to ensure that the long standing commitment to channel aid to the poorest becomes a reality. In the past British aid has been hardly more successful than that of multilateral institutions such as the World Bank in reaching the poor. This is especially true, as a recent War on Want publication has argued, of poor women. For too long the gender issue has been ignored by development planners, often with disastrous consequences in terms of increasing the exploitation of female labour and further marginalising women within the household and wider society. For an incoming Labour government the task of realising a poverty-focussed aid programme will pose formidable problems. However, its commitment to increasing the aid budget to 0.5% of gross domestic product (GDP) during the lifetime of the first parliament; upgrading the ODA to Cabinet status, and expanding its remit to oversee trade as well as aid co-operation; providing an institutional background capable of channelling aid to the poorest (including the establishment of special units to deal with women's issues) reflects the central demands of development NGOs and offers a framework for improvement.

Trade

While stressing the importance of the overseas aid programme, NGOs have also attempted to bring to public attention the critical role of international trade relations in determining the developing prospects of the Third World. In the past this meant advocacy of the commodity agreements envisaged in the IPC. Since the effective collapse of the North-South dialogue on this issue at UNCTAD in 1983, however, this has been less of a focal point. It might be added that, under the conditions of the 1980s (as the collapse of the rubber and tin agreements have underlined), the type of agreements envisaged by the IPC would not have provided effective insulation and price support to developing country exporters.

Although NGOs have continued their work on commodities, arguing in particular for international support to assist diversification away from primary commodity production and into processing, in recent years they have been increasingly concerned with the problem of protectionism. In all OECD countries the recession has been accompanied by a collapse of multilateral trade rules and

31

the erection of a bewildering array of tariff and non-tariff barriers. Despite its vehement commitment to market forces, the British Government has been no exception in this regard. Indeed, as a report of the Independent Group on British Aid has observed, "Britain is one of the most restrictive among the developed countries." This has been especially apparent in the textile trade, which is of enormous significance to several of the world's poorest nations. Under the Conservatives, Britain's Multi-Fibre Arrangement has been progressively tightened up during the renegotiations of 1981 and 1986.

Development NGOs have been at the forefront in demanding more liberal market access for the developing countries. One notable success was achieved, largely as a result of the lobbying work of the World Development Movement, when the British Government finally agreed to lift restrictions on imports of Bangladeshi shirts. For the most part, however, the protectionist tide has continued unabated, not least because of gathering trade tensions and structural imbalances between the three major OECD trading blocs; the US, the EC and Japan.

As a member state of the EC, British trade policy is determined to a significant degree, by deliberations in Brussels and the wider relationship between Europe and the South. Especially important in this regard is the Lomé Convention between the EC and sixty-six African, Caribbean and Pacific (ACP) states, thirty-eight of which are low income countries with a per capita GDP of less than $400. Development NGOs have long recognised the positive elements in the Lomé Convention, but have demanded radical improvements in its provisions. As a mechanism for promoting ACP exports, for example, the Lomé Convention has not been an outstanding success, with the ACP's share of European imports having fallen steadily over time. This has led NGOs to support the requests of the ACP countries for improved market access, in particular for the agricultural commodities

32

which make up the bulk of their exports. In terms of development aid, NGOs have also demanded improvements in the European Development Fund and compensatory finance facilities which have proven woefully inadequate in the face of the generalised financial crisis faced by the ACP countries.

Farm Policy and Food Security

One of the effects of the Ethiopian famine was to bring the question of food security to the heart of development education work in Britain. The fact that the famine itself occurred during a record cereals harvest in Europe gave an added poignancy. Images of bulging food stores in Europe and starving children in Ethiopia became a potent symbol of an international food system in a state of moral and economic anarchy.

One of the focal points of NGO work on the question of food security since 1985 has been the impact of the Common Agricultural Policy (CAP) on the developing countries. In November 1985, six major agencies issued a joint response to the EC Commission's Green Paper on CAP reform, demanding that development issues be brought into the reform debate. Four areas of special concern were outlined: 1) the cost of the CAP, which by absorbing two-thirds of the CAP budget prevented the development of a more substantial aid programme; 2) the tendency of the CAP, through its subsidised dumping of surplus produce on world markets, to reduce world prices and the export earnings of developing countries; 3) the costs of CAP protectionism to developing country exporters; 4) the dangers to developing country food security posed by CAP food dumping.

Since responding to the Green Paper, development NGOs have deepened their own understanding of the complex processes at work in the CAP and their impact on developing countries. The distressing account of the human costs of the EC's sugar dumping provided in Oxfam's book, *The Hunger Crop*, ought to be compulsory reading for all Eurocrats accustomed to justifying the unjustifiable by a mixture of incomprehensible CAP-speak and spurious economics. As *The Hunger Crop* shows, the EC's transition from a sugar importer to the world's largest exporter (solely on the basis of subsidised production and dumping) in a little over ten years, has had devastating human consequences for countries such as the Philippines and Jamaica. Unfortunately, the plight of malnourished children on the sugar-producing island of Negros in the Philippines has yet to figure on the Council of Ministers' CAP reform agenda, as witnessed by its recent refusal to countenance a cutback in production. Nonetheless, development agencies, united in the European Sugar Action Group, have continued to press for the cessation of European sugar exports and the participation of the Community in an International Sugar Agreement which supports world prices at reasonable levels.

As in the case of sugar, overproduction of EC cereals has serious consequences for developing countries. Because of overproduction in both the US and the EC, the world's agricultural superpowers, international cereal stocks are now equivalent to two years' annual trade levels. Moreover, prices have fallen to their lowest levels in real terms since the Great Depression and, with the EC and US locked in a subsidised dumping war, are set to continue their downward spiral. For small producers in developing countries, forced to compete with grain dumped in local markets at prices far below the cost of production, OECD cereal exports can spell ruin. The declining per-capita production of local staples in sub-Saharan Africa and parts of Latin America and alarming evolution of consumer habits in favour of cheap imported wheat cannot be separated from this process of surplus dumping. Nor can it be dissociated from the "cheap food" development strategies which, in many parts of the Third World, have marginalised the poor and resulted in the neglect of domestic agriculture. Indeed, the deadly inter-action of OECD food policies and the interests of nar-rowly based urban elites constitutes one of the major food security challenges of the 1980s.

Fundamentally, the food insecurity created by the CAP in developing countries is the result of an agricultural policy running out of control. The structural over-production of food in Europe is not only costly – some $20 billion in 1987 – but has caused widespread environ-mental damage and pollution from chemicals and pesti-cides. While big farms and giant chemical corporations such as ICI have benefited from the CAP, since they are the main recipients of its subsidies, the vast majority – consumers, taxpayers and small farmers alike – have not. This has led development NGOs to join with a wide range of other interest groups seeking CAP reform. Agen-cies such as the Catholic Institute for International Rela-tions (CIIR) and the World Development Movement, for example, have linked up with environmental, consumer and small-farmer organisations in demanding an end to subsidised over-production and export dumping.

However, while there may be agreement in principle on the problems associated with the CAP, there is less agreement on solutions. There is still an unfortunate tendency in Britain, on both the left and the right, to respond to any mention of the CAP with a knee-jerk "cut farm prices" reaction. In a country with a relatively small farm population and a farming structure dominated by highly capitalised big farms (operating at profit levels well in excess of the European average) this position has a certain populist respectability. For the majority of small farmers in Britain and elsewhere in Europe, however, sustained real price cuts would be devastating and result in mass bankruptcy. Moreover, in the face of ongoing productivity gains and with new biotechnological advances, it is doubtful whether price cuts alone will be capable of substantially reducing over-production. What is clear is that price cuts for farmers do not, as is often imagined, mean lower consumer prices. The main beneficiaries of lower farm prices are the giant food processing corporations for whom the 1980s have offered a profiteers' paradise.

What is required in Europe is rigorous control over agricultural output. That is, production quotas must be set at reasonable levels, taking into account Europe's own food requirements (as well as a range of social and environmental factors) and its relations with developing countries. Production in excess of quota should receive no price support, while the quotas themselves should be structured and distributed so as to support smaller farmers. This would at once end the cycle of over-production and dumping, reduce the capital intensity of farming and prevent European farming from undermining food security in developing countries. One of the major tasks of development NGOs as the CAP staggers from budgetary crisis to budgetary crisis, is to hammer home the point that there is no necessary conflict of interest between small farmers in the North and South. All agencies should unite in rejecting a supposedly free-market solution to the farm crisis, not least since its only long-term beneficiaries would be the handful of US corporations which control the grain trade, large-scale corporate farming enterprises and chemical input suppliers.

Development, Human Rights:
an NGO Perspective

It would be hard to find a more ideologically loaded term than "human rights", but since the 1960s, development agencies have been forced to confront the wide-ranging problems they pose. The point of departure for most agencies has been the Universal Declaration of Human Rights adopted by the UN in 1948, that "Everyone has a right to a standard of living adequate for the health and well-being of himself and his family, including food, clothing, and medical care and necessary social services". The implicit social content of this Declaration and its departure from narrowly defined liberal principles of individual rights, makes it especially relevant to the work of agencies in development projects involving Third World communities. But notably in the context of the present Cold War, where Western democracies deem it appropriate to sponsor international terrorist organisations in Nicaragua and elsewhere in the name of "individual freedom", work in the field of human rights has become increasingly fraught with political tensions and difficulties.

Growing recognition by NGOs that real development aid should empower the recipients and enable them to take control of their own lives, has forced them to distinguish between aid as "charity hand-outs" and aid as "partnership for growth". Fundamental to this distinction has been the influential, community-based education methods of Paulo Freire. These are designed to enable groups to confront local issues, come to grips with everyday problems and, in developing an understanding of the root causes of their poverty, pass from fatalism and apathy into analysis and action. This approach to development is political in the richest sense, with its potential for mobilising communities and promoting self-reliant development.

This approach also clearly draws NGOs into the political arena, particularly where popular struggles and efforts to mobilise confront repressive regimes. Liberal norms, oblivious to the fact that aid from governments is politically motivated, dictate that charities should stay out of politics. This is especially apparent in Britain where archaic charity laws preclude "political" activities, right down to an advertisement by Christian Aid advocating sanctions against South Africa. Under these circumstances the choice for NGOs is to either opt for "safe", "nonpolitical" projects (i.e. those falling broadly within the hand-out league) or risk attracting official ire by supporting projects which seek, through training and resources, to empower community groups and organisations. Further problems arise when these bodies are forced to bear the brunt of repression unleashed by regimes which see democratic organisation as a deadly threat – regimes which, as often as not, receive the political and economic support of Western (most notably the British and US) governments.

One of the most important tasks facing development NGOs in their educational work is the restoration of the contextual balance in the understanding of human rights. This formed the point of departure for a recent CIIR publication, *Right to Survive: Human Rights in Nicaragua*. In the context of a nation struggling to overthrow the historical structure of underdevelopment and poverty, the book argued, "basic human rights are logically and morally prior to the rest". While this might grate on the liberal conscience, such a point of departure represents an important challenge to the new right's "appropriation" of human rights as a tool for undermining the position of popular governments.

South Africa

In South Africa, the dilemmas and contradictions of liberal human rights approaches and development aid are at their most acute, for three reasons: the high level of Western investment, and its political influence, and historical linkages of Western governments (notably Britain, Germany and the United States) and the strength of mass-based, democratic organisation opposed to apartheid. No rational approach to development in South Africa can avoid giving priority to the elimination of apartheid. The struggle allows no middle ground, simply various arenas of conflict. Where the mass-based, voteless democratic organisations of the black communities bring pressures for change from below, they confront a mixture of naked state violence, ranging from vigilantes to the police and army, to legalised repression in the form of detention without trial, bannings and restrictions. The other side of the repression coin, "reform", appropriates the language of democracy while depriving it of content. This "moderate" voice is constantly echoed by the British Prime Minister, Mrs Thatcher, with a singular lack of embarrassment in order to counterdemand applying sanctions and other measures to bring apartheid to an end. While the communities in which NGO projects are rooted – the civic associations, youth organisations, trade unions, church groups – call for Britain to use its economic muscle against South Africa and force the Botha Government to the negotiating table, Mrs Thatcher's programme of "positive measures" includes reduced aid to the beleaguered frontline states, and selective educational aid to black South Africans. Western support for Chief Buthelezi, chief minister of the "homeland government" of Kwazulu, is nowhere warmer than in Britain and West Germany. This is despite the fact that Buthelezi's Inkatha movement is at the heart of a violent bid for control in Natal townships and has supported the apartheid state in flagrantly violating the human rights of South Africans. It will come as no surprise that Buthelezi's appeal is that he opposes sanctions and supports big business.

The homelands themselves expose some of the painful

decisions of development funders, which only clear criteria based on political analysis can resolve. These areas, some of them designated "independent", are the dumping ground of apartheid, under the control of repressive surrogates of the Pretoria government. Here, supporting destitute people can also mean providing active reinforcement for the South African government's policy of segregation and forced population removals. These homelands feature in a wider national and international economic pattern. Attracted by incentives from a government desperate to spread the burden of paying for apartheid, a new wave of investors, headed by countries like Taiwan, are setting up factories and reaping the advantages of low-paid, non-unionised labour subject to brutal state repression. In South Africa generally, P.W. Botha's economic policies sound like home from home to British business: he has embarked on a massive programme of privatisation and deregulation, from bus companies which transport workers from distant settlements to housing townships which are being "upgraded" as part of apartheid's modifications.

The temerity of South Africans who believed that they should control their own future and development created a minor crisis in the EC in 1987 which had begun funding NGO projects in South Africa while ducking the sanctions issue. The South Africans, through the churches and a secular body called the Kagiso Trust, negotiated conditions for accepting EC development funds: broadly, these required that they would be used only for furthering development in the context of a democratic process of liberation from apartheid. The EC, seeking an alibi for pusillanimity, agreed but later came under pressure from Britain and other member-states to refuse projects involving political organisation including a National Youth Congress. In the event, the NGOs refused to drop projects considered politically "contentious" and won the stand-off.

South African organisations have played a major role in setting the agenda for British NGOs. In their world, politics involves clear choices, with ordinary people denied the luxury of neutrality. Non-government agencies concerned with real human rights, democracy and development have also been forced to either take sides in the struggle against apartheid or stay at home. While the political struggle for the future of South Africa is rooted in the townships development agencies have also to continue a struggle in their own backyard. In particular they need to confront the hypocrisy of official opposition to sanctions and to counter the quiescent British media's refusal to communicate the realities of apartheid to the general public.

Debt and Structural Adjustment

For the South, and in particular the poorest and most vulnerable sections of its population, the foreign debt burden is the most serious symptom of a generalised economic crisis. This crisis can, in important respects, be traced back to disastrous domestic development policies. Throughout Latin America and Africa import substitution growth models, supported by overvalued exchange rates, resulted in sharply deteriorating trade balances during the late 1960s and 1970s. These were exacerbated by the oil price hikes of 1973 and 1979, with the ensuing current account deficits being covered by foreign borrowing. During the late 1970s, especially in Latin America, attempts were made to counter the failures of import substitution by restructuring local economies and opening them to free-market forces. This, however, succeeded mainly in blowing away the fragile gains of the past two decades. Moreover, because of its political and social requirements, the free-market model was typically implemented by right-wing military dictatorships. These were not slow to take advantage of political power by engaging in an armaments spending-spree financed largely by overseas bankers and governments.

The gathering development crisis of the 1970s was obscured to some extent by the low real interest rates and abundant commercial bank loans of the period. Developing countries became prime lending targets for commercial banks anxious to recycle OPEC oil funds but faced with restricted outlets at home because of the industrial recession. The bubble burst in 1979/80, as rigid monetarist policies in the North forced up world interest rates and threw the OECD economies into reverse gear. The convergence of high real interest rates (which rose from negative levels to over 21% between 1980/82) and the collapsing commodity prices which resulted from the economic downturn in the OECD countries, crippled the developing countries. Forced to finance an increasing debt service burden from a dwindling foreign exchange base, they became trapped in a vicious circle of borrowing increasing amounts of capital simply to meet past interest payments. Although interest rates have fallen since 1982 they remain at exceptionally high levels, especially if measured against developing country commodity export prices. During the period 1980/85 primary commodity prices fell by some 5% per annum, implying an annual average foreign exchange loss of $8 billion. Despite the faltering recovery in the North, the primary commodity price index fell by a further 10% in 1985 and 1986. The continued deterioration in commodity prices and terms of trade in 1986–7 has been especially severe for sub-Saharan Africa which lost some $19 billion *more* than the combined total of official development assistance and commercial bank lending.

As the ability of developing countries to service their debt has diminished, capital inflows from the North have slowed dramatically. The result has been a net outflow of capital from some of the world's most impoverished nations. Between 1982 and 1985 Latin America transferred between $47 and $76 billion in capital to the North. In 1985 Brazil alone transferred $11 billion to its commercial bank creditors, equivalent to 5% of its GDP. Although there is still a small net inflow into sub-Saharan Africa, this fell from $2.7 billion to $0.8 billion between 1980 and 1985.

In order to facilitate this transfer of resources, many developing countries have been forced to reduce their imports and maintain large current account surpluses. Overall, the world's fifteen most heavily indebted countries cut the volume of their imports by 10% per annum between 1982 and 1985. But this import squeeze is only part of a wider contraction of savings, investment and consumption. Instead of nourishing local industry and agriculture, Third World savings are being transferred to Western banks, placing their longer-term recovery in jeopardy. Under the auspices of IMF/World Bank lending programmes, wages have been forced down while currency devaluation and the removal of government subsidies on basic items (the twin planks of most structural adjustment programmes) have forced up the cost of living. In many cases, as underlined by UNICEF research, the inevitable result has been increased unemployment, declining nutritional status and rising levels of infant mortality. As Oxfam's book, *For Richer for Poorer*, puts it:

> The highest price for the debt crisis is being paid for by the world's poor; by those who can least afford to pay. Their wages (if they have been able to keep jobs) have fallen steeply in relation to costs of living. The cost of their basic foods has soared as, for instance, government subsidies have been lifted. Expenditure on health care, education and other social service systems has been cut back. The international problem of recession has become, in its cruellest manifestation, a crisis of hunger for millions.

The parallels with certain manifestations of social crisis in Britain itself are readily apparent, though most NGOs (in part because of the political constraints under which they operate) have not used this analogy as a platform upon which to build their educational work. For the most part, this has been directed towards informing public opinion about three areas of the debt crisis where the British Government has considerable international influence: 1) commercial bank debt 2) official debt and 3) structural adjustment.

Commercial Bank Debt

British high-street banks, having expanded their lending to today's highly indebted countries by some 60% per annum during the late 1970s, are major actors on the Third World debt scene. In 1985/6 their overall lending to the Third World stood at some $40 billion, with the lion's share in Latin America. In the case of the four main clearing banks, exposure to Latin America now accounts for between 70% and 100% of their net assets. Income from interest on Latin American loans was equivalent to between 50% and 100% of their pre-tax profits between 1982 and 1985, the major share being held by Midlands and Lloyds. As War on Want's educational work in its "Profits out of Poverty" campaign has emphasised, the Latin American poor bear a disproportionate part of the burden of meeting these repayments. This places a responsibility upon the British Government and public to create structures which ensure that their banks cease to be part of the poor's problem, rather than part of the solution to a largely self-inflicted crisis.

Since 1982 NGOs have been increasingly involved in the debate over the problem of debt reform. All the major agencies would agree upon the need for longer-term rescheduling and interest-rate capping in order to reduce the level of debt service payments. They would also concur in advocating that new commercial bank loans be made available, where necessary with government backing, in addition to increased multilateral transfers. While stopping short of the Cuban proposal that developing countries consider outright default, many agencies have similarly urged substantial debt forgiveness and cancellation.

Over the past eighteen months, the debt reform agenda has itself been radicalised by the toughening stance of developing countries. Although debtor groupings, such as the Cartegena Group in Latin America, have yet to exercise debtor power collectively, the debt-service ceilings set by Peru and Nigeria have had important knock-on effects. This has recently been underlined at major debtor conferences in both sub-Saharan Africa and Latin America, where demands for repayment ceilings and interest-rate capping have been widely supported. By far the most important unilateral debtor action to date, however, has been the Brazilian debt repayment moratorium announced in February 1987. This has exercised a profound effect on debt rescheduling negotiations and the creditor-debtor dialogue, not least since it provoked a series of commercial bank loss provisions against their Third World debts. These implicitly recognised what had long been apparent: namely that a substantial portion of Third World debt will never be repaid and that the banks, their shareholders and governments will have to share in the burden of adjustment.

Development agencies have built upon this breakthrough by arguing, in a language the British Government understands, that the market itself now dictates the need for a large scale write-off of commercial bank debt. In its *World Development Crisis*, for example, the Catholic Institute for International Relations (CIIR) pointed out that, with developing country debt typically changing hands on the secondary market at less than half face value and provisions being made against the loss of up to a third of total lending, banks themselves have started to come to terms with the realities of the market. So far, however, they have refused to translate accounting practices into their repayment arrangements. This is hardly surprising, given the fact that writing off between a quarter and half of Latin American debt alone would cost from $5 billion to $10 billion. Moreover, since most of them are now sitting on swingeing potential losses – accumulated as a result of deregulation on the stock market and the stockpiling of Eurobonds to finance a consumer credit boom – they are unlikely to carry through a substantial write-off themselves. This places an onus on the British Government to use its substantial excess revenues to finance an orderly write-down. To date it has refused to countenance this step on the grounds that it would force up public-sector borrowing and generate inflationary pressures – sacrilege in terms of the monetarist bible. In reality, however, with the revenues generated by the privatisation of public assets having sharply reduced public-sector borrowing requirements, substantial action could be taken without serious borrowing or inflationary implications. As regards the longer-term stability of the banking system and the interests of the public, a state sponsored write-down of Third World debt is eminently preferable to tax cuts designed to increase the wealth of a small minority. This point has been cogently argued by War on Want, but it is also worth noting that whatever the short-term costs for the British taxpayer, the present costs of debt servicing for the Third World are considerably greater. As the CIIR has argued:

> While there would clearly be economic costs in any large-scale write-off, it is important to set these in perspective. Taking the main creditor countries as a group, writing off $300 million of their banks' Third

World debt holdings over a five-year period would absorb only 1% of their GDP per annum (or 7% of their collective military budgets). This pales into insignificance against the costs currently being borne by the debtor countries.

Official Debt

Turning to official debt, which accounts for the overwhelming bulk of the total in sub-Saharan Africa, the British Government's response has been more encouraging. Under the terms of the so-called Lawson Initiative announced at an IMF meeting in spring 1987, it has continued the practice (initiated by the Labour Government in 1978 under the Retrospective Terms Adjustment) of converting Overseas Development Administration (ODA) loans into grants – effectively writing them off. Other countries, most significantly Canada, have recently followed Britain's lead in this area, though much remains to be done. To date, less than $6 billion has been written off internationally, and the US and Japan have hardly begun the process of converting loans to grants.

The Lawson Initiative also advocated reducing real interest rates for the poorest countries by providing subsidised credit. This idea was discussed at the OECD's Venice Summit in 1987, but effectively blocked by the US and West Germany. Development agencies have strongly supported the Government's efforts to persuade its OECD partners to find appropriate means of reducing real interest rates. But they have also pointed out some of the acute contradictions which the Lawson Initiative has highlighted in terms of the Government's overall debt strategy. For example, as we noted above, it has refused to consider writing off commercial bank debt despite the fact that middle-income debtors are no less insolvent than the low-income countries in which official credit is concentrated. Admittedly, commercial debt does raise a different set of questions for the international financial system. But it would seem pointless to provide developing countries with more resources through official debt relief and increased multilateral lending while capital outflows are continued through interest payments to private creditors. Another source of concern has been the Government's refusal to support the principle of converting World Bank and IMF loans into grants. In view of the fact that the World Bank has acknowledged that several of the poorest countries will never repay their outstanding debt and that the IMF is currently a *net recipient* of funds from sub-Saharan Africa, this can only be described as myopic.

When announcing his "Initiative" at the IMF, the British Chancellor, Nigel Lawson, complained of a weakening in the conditionality of its lending policies. For those subjected to its structural adjustment packages, this might have come as some surprise. But for British NGOs the Government's rigid adherence to the standard structural adjustment formula – liberalise, devalue, deflate and wait for the OECD economies to drag the world economy into sustained growth – presents a major challenge. At the most obvious level, it is difficult to argue (especially in the "non-political" discourse forced upon development agencies) that the Government ought not to be recommending overseas precisely the type of free-market policies it is committed to at home.

To some extent, the publication of the United Nations Children's Fund (UNICEF)'s *Adjustment With a Human Face* has shifted the agenda both within Britain and internationally. Its demand for welfare criteria to be given more emphasis in the formulation and implementation of adjustment packages has recently been taken on board at the rhetorical level by both the IMF and the World Bank. Whether this will mean more than the latter's empty commitments of the 1970s to shift the focus of its aid to the "poorest of the poor" remains to be seen, though there is little evidence of a marked policy shift to date. The British Government too has declared itself in favour of many of UNICEF's prescriptions, not least since it is well aware that political gestures to the development lobby cost little and can bring considerable public relations benefits.

Within the development agencies there is universal agreement that adjustment with a human face would be infinitely preferable to the ongoing holocaust being suffered by the poor in developing countries. Several of the major agencies involved in dialogue with the World Bank and the IMF have used the UNICEF proposals to lobby for basic reforms in the implementation of adjustment packages. But the problems associated with structural adjustment go far deeper than the social welfare effects of IMF/World Bank conditionality. Fundamentally, structural adjustment is premised upon social and economic assumptions about the recovery process and the very *purpose* of economic growth which development agencies should reject. Firstly, its advocacy of externally oriented recovery when there is clear evidence that world economic growth is slowing (and no evidence that even optimal growth scenarios will result in sustained commodity price increases or reduced debt service ratios) is a clear recipe for deepening economic crisis. Secondly, its insistence upon deflation through the mechanisms of trade and domestic consumption is economically suicidal and socially catastrophic for the Third World. Most developing countries are presently suffering enormous economic inefficiency and lost production as a result of local industries operating below capacity because of infrastructural collapse, limited credit and lack of domestic demand. What is required in these cases is controlled reflation and, where necessary, the protection of local industries from imports.

Leaving aside its legion of internal contradictions, IMF/
World Bank structural adjustment is based upon the view
that economic growth *per se* is good. Dressed up in the
detached "non-political" technocratic language of market
economists, it embodies deeply political assumptions.
Perhaps most importantly, it embodies the assumption
that economic growth governed solely by free-market
forces is the proper measure of social welfare, the universal panacea for poverty and the only rational means of
optimising production and distributing income. In the
Britain of the 1980s the shallow deception of such economic "theory" as well as its class content, has become
all too apparent. While some sections of the country and
some regions have benefited from the recent economic
growth, the growing polarisation of society, deepening
poverty and marginalisation of groups such as the unemployed, women and blacks tell an important story: the
expansion of the City of London and consumer booms
centred on the shires and the South of England, have not
and will not "trickle down" to those most in need.

Development agencies have long been well aware of
this reality in their overseas work and have played a part
in demanding the fundamental political and social
changes which would be needed to convert economic
growth into a generalised improvement in human welfare. Perhaps their greatest challenge as we enter the
second decade of Thatcherism is for them to play a fuller
part in exposing the myths of economic growth models
at home and abroad which regard human welfare criteria
and distribution as irrelevant non-market side issues.
Along with other bodies working to support the poor at
home, NGOs must work to restore these issues to their
proper place in economic planning. In short, they need to
demand the subordination of economics to people politics
and morality both in Britain and in our contacts with the
developing world. As the Church of England's *Faith in
the City Report* argued, unbridled commitment to the

free market and rampant individualism are not conducive to the pursuit of the common good, either at home or abroad:

> The main assumption on which present economic policies are based is that prosperity can be restored if individuals are set free to pursue their own economic salvation. The appeal is to economic self-interest and individualism ... (but) ... in the absence of a spirit of collective obligation or the collective will to foster it, there is no guarantee that the pursuit of innumerable individual self-interests will add up to improvement of the common good.

Privatisation and the Voluntary Sector: Dangers North and South

NIGEL TWOSE
PRISCILLA ANNAMANTHODO

Nigel Twose has been a member of the Labour Party for eighteen years. He has worked with NGOs for the last twelve years; from 1979–83 he worked with Oxfam in West Africa and was based in Burkina Faso. He currently works with the Panos Institute, an information and policy studies institute, as Co-Director of their Sahel programme. He is married to Priscilla Annamanthodo. They have two children and live in the North London borough of Brent.

Priscilla Annamanthodo works on local economic issues in Brent with the Local Economy Resource Unit. She has previously worked for Brent Council, particularly with black-managed community organisations, and on anti-racism with the Councils for Voluntary Service National Association. While living in West Africa, she worked with a women's training project in the Sahel.

Privatisation has been one of the most striking features of Britain under Margaret Thatcher. It has been a powerful weapon in the hands of the Conservative Government as it has sought to deprive local government of much of its power.

One aspect of its overall strategy has been to create a greater role for certain parts of the voluntary sector. It appears that the same process is now taking place in the South: Northern-dominated international structures and donor governments are seeking to reduce the power of national governments and are promoting a greater role for non-governmental organisations.

It is premature to draw definitive conclusions from the British experience. But it is our belief that a greater understanding of events in Britain may help us all to decide on the most appropriate response to developments in Africa.

In this article, we shall look at the parallels in the way the privatisation process is being applied in the North and in the South, giving examples from inner city London on the one hand and from the Sahel zone of Africa on the other. By voluntary organisations or non-governmental organisations (NGOs), we mean organisations which may employ staff and have a reasonably well-defined structure (thus distinguishing themselves from most informal institutions), but which do not work for profit and do not constitute part of the system of state service provision.

There is nothing wrong with an enlarged role for

voluntary movements – both authors have spent many years working in the voluntary sector. But we believe that the type of role which is being encouraged is an inappropriate one. We also fear that in the long run it may prove to be damaging to some of the most important aspects of voluntary sector work.

The North

Much of the recent debate about the voluntary sector and privatisation in Britain was triggered by a speech in 1984 by the then Secretary of State for Social Services, Norman Fowler. The Buxton Speech, as it came to be known, outlined a role for Social Services Departments as facilitators and service planners; the actual provision of services could be transferred into the hands of the private and voluntary sectors. The promised Green Paper never materialised, but the new onslaught of privatisation forced on local authorities has reawakened memories of that earlier suggestion.

These proposals for a new voluntary sector/statutory sector relationship were received ambivalently. Some certainly welcomed an expansion of voluntary provision: the statutory sector was supposedly too rigid, bureaucratic, expensive, slow and unresponsive. The voluntary sector in its myriad forms was seen as responsive, cheap, flexible and innovatory. More involvement by the voluntary sector in welfare provision had to be a good development.

And in many cases, this has proved to be the reality. Many local authorities with large black and minority populations, for example, were forced to realise that a number of services, for which they were responsible, were provided in ways that had been inaccessible to many of their black residents; a natural and positive response was to fund voluntary organisations which

56

would be able to provide more effective services. But it is important to note that these voluntarily provided services were paralleled by efforts to make council services more accessible to more communities: the local authorities' long-term responsibilities were never challenged.

What is now being actively discussed is a more systematic change, in which voluntary organisations, with the support of central government and certain local authorities, would play a far more important role.

The voluntary sector and the state are intimately bound together by the funding which the state makes available at both central and local level. The latest figures show that grants from statutory bodies now represent the largest single source of income for registered charities: from £576.9 million in 1980 to £1,375 million in 1985. The level of central government support has also increased by 91% in real terms, from £93.1 million in 1980 to £268 million in 1986.

By far the largest source of support comes from quangos like the Manpower Services Commission, whose support to the voluntary sector now equals that received from all other government sources. More than half the 244,000 Community Programme places will be filled by voluntary sector schemes. For example, the National Association for the Care and Resettlement of Offenders (NACRO)'s deep involvement with the Community Programme has led to it being described as an "arm of the state".

It is important to begin any discussion by recognising the implications of this increasing financial and ideological encouragement for the voluntary sector. We strongly believe that the voluntary sector in Britain is likely to expand, with increasing importance being attached to commercial qualities such as marketing. This movement into a different financial world, with priority attached to market share and a stake in the system, will further marginalise the non-service voluntary sector such as campaigning and advocacy groups. "Focussing on marketing, on advertising, on professional fund-raising and consultancy will concentrate power in the hands of fewer and fewer large organisations." (S. Etherington, "Heading for the Big Time", *Insight*, November 1987.)

The first question that has to be asked is one of feasibility: what position is the voluntary sector in to meet the challenge? Even potential supporters for a greater voluntary sector role recognise that the "voluntary sector as currently constituted and structured, has only a limited capacity to administer and regulate any significant transfer of provision from the statutory sector". (D. Leat, "Privatisation and Voluntarisation". *Quarterly Journal of Social Affairs*, 1986, 2 (3).)

Many voluntary agencies are extremely anxious about expanded responsibilities – even with increased funding. A 1986 study showed that many agencies feared they would be forced to develop structurally in ways which were not necessarily their own priority, because this was a condition of continued funding. Their view was that any radical restructuring and redesign of their current roles could well undermine their foundations and their grassroots community origins, thus weakening the very characteristics which define the voluntary sector.

The second area of concern is one of economic advantage: it should not be assumed that the voluntary sector can necessarily do everything cheaper than the state sector. There is "no good reason for supposing voluntary activity to be cost effective except in the crude financial sense that volunteers do not have to be paid". (R. Sugden, "Voluntary Organisations and the Welfare State", *Privatisation and the Welfare State*, edited by J. Le Grand and R. Robinson, Allen and Unwin, 1984.)

And significant questions of principle are raised if the voluntary sector is to provide value for money through more unpaid volunteers. Although volunteers make an invaluable contribution through the gift of their time and talents, it would be hard to imagine a complex professional service which relied primarily on this kind of staffing. Any attempts to introduce contracts of "employment" with specific job descriptions would undermine the very basis of volunteering. And efforts to link community service with jobs and training through the Community Programme will certainly be undermined by forthcoming moves to make the whole scheme compulsory, paying little more than basic unemployment benefit.

It is also difficult to imagine that an adequate supply of volunteers will be available in the areas where they are most needed. Research has shown that need does not necessarily produce a high voluntary response. There also seems to be a strong correlation between involvement in voluntary work and class, so that in areas of greatest deprivation voluntary activity does not automatically rise up to fulfil local need (nor to plug any holes in the statutory sector).

But perhaps more important in the long term than any of these arguments about comparative advantage is the "tendency if not the purpose of welfare pluralist accounts – to depoliticise the welfare issues with which they are concerned". (Beresford and Croft "Welfare Pluralism, the New Face of Fabianism", *Critical Social Policy*, 1984, 19.) By focussing the voluntary sector's involvement on questions of service provision, the underlying analysis of factors which created the need for welfare services is underplayed. The social and economic origins of these needs are relegated to second place; the voluntary sector's lobbying role is marginalised; political connections are lost.

In an environment of increasing pressure on many local authorities, it may occasionally be almost tempting for them to surrender part of their responsibilities. But in the context of a fast-eroding welfare state, any attempts to reduce local government's responsibilities *vis-à-vis* their constituents must surely be challenged.

This is not to imply that local state services are by definition better for the consumer. In fact, in many cases there is deep dissatisfaction with council provision: in social services, in housing, in education. And it is this discontent which has eased the way for the private schemes which are able to ignore the needs of all those without economic power.

As yet, it is too early to see what the real impact of the new privatisation legislation will be on the relationship between the voluntary sector and local authorities. However, there are indicative developments, like the relationship being worked on between Westminster Council and the local voluntary agency, Age Concern. Age Concern already provide ten day-centres for elderly people and the plan is to develop a much clearer contractual relationship between the council and the agency. The local authority's social workers will be able to buy in specific services for their clients from Age Concern. There are clearly potential advantages for customer services in this arrangement, but it is worrying to consider what might happen to the important advocacy role of an organisation which becomes bound so closely to a funding council.

Despite this range of concerns, there are many voluntary organisations which will be more than willing to take on an expanded role. Paradoxically, they are likely to come from very different ends of the political spectrum. At one end are the traditional service-oriented groups, who will simply see this growth as more of the same. At the other end there are black and minority organisations who still think, and often with good cause, that the local council is incapable of offering the right kinds of services to their communities, and who want to retain and expand their role.

Another dimension which must be added to the complexities of the current situation is the financial quagmire in a number of inner city boroughs and their relationship with central government. Government restrictions on spending have made it inevitable that authorities, particularly poor authorities with relatively low rates incomes, have had little more than one of two choices: potential imprisonment for not setting a budget which central government considers legal; or cuts in services. Many have chosen cuts – and of course the voluntary sector has not been exempted. This involves some very difficult decisions which authorities have approached in different ways.

At the time of writing, final decisions have not yet been made about how grant aid and other support to the voluntary sector will be cut. Some local authorities like Islington are looking at how to make "fair cuts", rather than across-the-board reductions. The council is evaluating groups in terms of how well they meet the three council priorities of providing direct services, combating poverty and promoting equal opportunities.

Camden councillors decided that the voluntary sector should face the same level of cuts as the council itself – 20%. It has prioritised support to those groups providing direct client "front line" services, and also said that organisations working with under-fives and those working against racism will be given high priority.

Lewisham is hoping to take a strategic approach to its cuts through evaluating usage of services.

But whichever decision councils reach, it is clear that campaigning and development organisations will be given the lowest priority for funding. The result is that the voluntary sector will lose some of its most radical and outspoken local voices, voices that are critical in the struggle to maintain local services. Black groups will also be particularly vulnerable, as they are especially dependent on public funding.

In the current environment of cuts and local contraction, it may seem contradictory to suggest that the voluntary sector is set to expand. But we must look at which authorities are being forced into cuts by government policies: primarily Labour authorities in poor inner city areas. It seems that the government considers it wise to weaken the existing constitution before the voluntary sector can be reshaped.

The South

The parallels in process between this British experience and the rapidly evolving situation in Africa are striking.

At the beginning of 1988, a week-long conference in Khartoum slowly pieced together the different theoretical roles of NGOs and the state. Most participants argued that objectives were ultimately the same, but all agreed that the approach of NGOs and that of government differs – and that it is right that it should differ.

Government is about policy formation and control, but it is also about providing the people with the resources and services they need to participate in the development of their community. In contrast, NGOs may seek an input into policy formation, but they should not be primarily about service delivery. They are "mechanisms to let the people's voice be heard". They are about empowerment, about recognising and mobilising the skills within the community. "It is not for us NGOs to specify even what the grassroots approaches will be. We must discover them with the people."

But if that conference managed to distinguish complementary roles, the reality today is a risk that the roles will become increasingly blurred in just the way we outlined above for Britain.

In 1981, the World Bank's "Accelerated Development in the Sub-Saharan Africa" argued strongly in favour of the intrinsic virtue of free-market mechanisms. Three years later, its report "Toward Sustained Development in Sub-Saharan Africa" developed the argument, stating that "the respective roles of the central government, local governments, community and co-operative groups, and the private sector need to be examined, and in many cases the balance needs to be altered if a more efficient use of resources is to be achieved".

"In most African countries," it argued, "public sector responsibilities and employment have become unmanageably large. Whilst the public sector's responsibilities for easing Africa's basic constraints are set to grow, some of them can be carried out more efficiently by community efforts and the private sector . . . The issue is not whether to favor the public or the private sector in the abstract; it is how to reduce the burden on the public sector and encourage the private sector in a way that provides the services more efficiently and is consistent with national priorities."

As a condition for continued funding, borrowing countries are increasingly being required to implement certain basic economic reforms. In particular, governments are being urged to allow the private sector to enjoy a greater role in their economies. The privatists argue the need to transfer ownership from public to private and, with that, the need to move towards greater competition.

In the African Sahel (the ecological zone stretching from Mauritania and Senegal in the west across to Somalia in the east), nine of the eleven countries are currently undertaking market-oriented reform. At the time of writing, only Burkina Faso and Ethiopia have resisted. But the downturn in the world economy and lower commodity export prices means an even greater influence for the views put forward by the IMF, the World Bank and the major bilateral donors.

Measures designed to reduce public expenditure and to increase the scope of the private sector have become almost standard features of the package which Sahelian governments are under pressure to implement. The World Bank argues that during this process of "adjustment", there are two ways of protecting the poor. One is to redirect existing social expenditures to ensure that they are cost effective and focussed on the poor; they suggest charging people for curative health services, for example, and using the funds to subsidise preventative health services. The other way is to use quite separate funds to compensate the poor directly – and here the Bank advocates an increased role for the voluntary sector. In contrast to government, NGOs are presented as low cost, committed, flexible and efficient.

It is not our intention to analyse the World Bank's adjustment strategy here, but to look at the relationship in roles being advocated for Sahelian government and for the Sahelian voluntary sector.

It is important to stress that not all NGO activities are being encouraged. The Bank's NGO support appears to be effectively restricted to compensatory programmes for the poor. In exactly the same spirit, Michael Camdessus, Managing Director of the IMF, said in Nairobi in November 1987 that "we must recognise the devoted contribution of non-governmental organisations in directly alleviating the plight of the poor". Not a mention of NGO involvement in long-term development or campaigning, just a phrase reminiscent of a dictionary definition of social work.

Claude Cheysson is a member of the European Commission with responsibility for North/South relations. He says that "at the World Bank, the OECD (Organisation for Economic Co-operation and Development), the European Commission, the Ministries for Co-operation in the industrialised countries, people are now examining NGO methods, studying the possibility of transposing co-operation programmes . . . But there are other avenues to explore. NGOs could be involved in larger scale operations financed chiefly from public funds, with the authorities providing the infrastructure and the NGOs ensuring the progress in the field. Or again, one could subsidise the NGOs by topping up their own resources, without in any way reducing their independence or interfering with their methods of operating." It is exactly this kind of statement, however flattering, which may make NGOs unaware of the way in which they run the risk of becoming unwitting stooges in the process of taking power away from Southern governments.

The EEC and the Bank are not alone in promoting this process: NGOs have become one of the current priorities of the United Nations Development Programme (along with women and the private sector); the United Nations High Commission for Refugees has programmes for 12 million refugees around the world – one third of these are now run by NGOs; USAID has 30 million dollars this year for NGOs in Somalia; the Somali NGO movement only began within the last few years, and there are just five of them functioning.

This level of enthusiasm and financial support needs to be seen in the context of *reduced* financial support to African governments. None of this funding is additional money: NGO income is currently the only area of resource growth in Africa. It is not surprising that increasing numbers of African governments view it with concern.

Look at the example of Sudan. At the height of the famine in 1985, weekly situation meetings were held in Khartoum's Hilton Hotel, chaired by a United Nations representative, with the different NGOs giving reports on the number of people fed in each region and the amount of additional food required. Many of the NGOs clearly relished their new-found power, while Sudanese government officials sat around the edge of the meeting room, taking notes, forced into the role of impotent observers.

At a symposium in London in March 1987, the delegate from the Sudan Council of Churches stated very clearly that African governments see NGOs competing with them for funds. "NGOs are trusted, while governments are reduced to being spectators. . ." His views were echoed nearly a year later at the Khartoum conference by the Director of the Islamic African Relief Agency, Dr Abdella Suleiman: "When we go for funds to UN organisations, the Government is our biggest competitor".

That rapid expansion of the NGO sector in Sudan at the expense of government intervention was precipitated by the drought and famine of 1984/85. In Burkina Faso, though, the balance was changed for clearly political considerations.

When the Government of the late Thomas Sankara came to power in 1983, Northern donors were nervous of the revolutionary rhetoric but fascinated by the innovative approaches to development work. The solution was predictable: cut back bilateral funding to the state and increase funding through NGOs. Burkina had been an adventure playground for NGOs since the mid-seventies, with minimal state involvement, but by 1986 the situation had become disastrous. Chris Roche of Liverpool University calculates that bilateral aid dropped by 25 million dollars over the three-year period, while assistance through NGOs increased by 17 million dollars. No authority could tolerate such a crude mechanism to bypass its own role in development planning, and few people were surprised that the Government introduced a range of measures to co-ordinate the work of the voluntary sector.

We can follow the story more closely with the reasonably well-developed case study of neighbouring Mali. Back in the autumn of 1981, the Malian Government agreed to a programme of market-oriented economic reform, including privatisation of state enterprises, as a condition of continued funding. That programme has moved ahead with speed, and one consequence has been a reduction in state employment (all students were previously guaranteed employment).

The entrepreneurial initiative which such measures are presumably designed to encourage has manifested itself in Mali through the creation of ever larger numbers of Malian NGOs. Many of them are set up by the civil servants who have been laid off and staffed by the students who have failed to get a job. But it is important to note that these are not NGOs in the sense of popular groupings at community level: instead, they represent a new private-sector alternative. In consequence, we now see a European Government giving money to a European NGO which hands it over to a new Malian NGO which then gives whatever is left to a community initiative. It is a crystal-clear example of Northern donors removing a Sahelian government from certain spheres of involvement and giving NGOs the money to intervene in their place.

The boundary lines are becoming blurred in the most surprising places. Norway may be one of the most progressive aid donors, but these same political pressures in favour of the private sector have resulted in the rapid growth of Norwegian consultancy companies. For the most part, they are heavily profit making, and were often specifically established to soak up government aid money. In a direct parallel with Mali, many of these consultancy companies are staffed by people who used to work in the aid ministry – to the increasing disquiet of large numbers of people.

Conclusion

We believe that the voluntary sector needs to grow, both in the North and in the South. This article should not be interpreted as an argument for not funding voluntary organisations. It is no more than an attempt to point out the potential dangers in current growth trends.

Along with many of our colleagues, we would challenge the view that almost everything is done better by the private sector, in Britain or in Africa. Goods and services regularly need to be produced and distributed in accordance with criteria other than value-for-money, and we are fearful at the looming prospect of voluntary organisations offering competitive tenders for sub-contracted social service provision.

Government is not entirely incompetent, as some ideologues would have us believe. And voluntary organisations are not all super-efficient structures either. It should not be a question of choosing between the state and the voluntary sector; we must recognise that both have different and necessary roles.

Despite calls by groups like One World for an international vision, there is a continuing tendency to see events in the North and the South as separate and unlinked. We must begin by recognising some of the common processes which affect us: the British voluntary sector is considerably stronger than the African NGO movement, but it is striking to note the comparative ease with which both are being co-opted. We all need to be aware of this dominant conservative perception of the state as something inherently bad, which must therefore be minimised.

Any structure takes decisions on the basis of survival and growth: as funding sources for certain areas of activity dry up, many voluntary organisations are now facing terminal cuts. But the voluntary sector must be cautious about any change in its structure as a whole and, in particular, about potential shifts in the relationship with the state.

Swords to Ploughshares

MICHAEL MANLEY

Michael Manley served as Prime Minister of Jamaica from 1972 to 1980. He has, since 1967, been an MP in Kingston and is currently Leader of the Opposition. He is a noted historian and writer and has worked as a freelance journalist for the BBC. His books include *The Politics of Change*, *A Voice at the Workplace*, *The Search for Solutions*, *Up the Down Escalator* and, most recently, *A History of West Indies Cricket*.

The two most familiar statistics in today's world are the trillion dollars which are spent each year on arms and the trillion dollars which the countries of the Third World or the South owe to the banks of the countries of the first world or the North. In simplistic terms, each figure reflects the end product of a kind of collective insanity, a derangement in the international process. More realistically, both figures are the logical outcome of historical forces which it is our duty to reverse.

Any discussion on the critical issues of world politics is assisted if the protagonists declare their personal positions at the outset. I believe that the world needs desperately a system of collective security as an umbrella for general phased disarmament. I believe that the world needs a system of management to ensure that the global economy is restructured to provide equitable opportunity for the development of the nations of the South.

Of course, it is obvious that a fraction of the resources now devoted to death by some nations of the North could help create the conditions for life for all nations, and particularly for those of the South. However, what is less obvious is that the failure to disarm is associated with the same forces which block the effort to restructure and, hence, that disarmament and development are inseparably linked.

We can safely dismiss the claims of those who seek to mystify present defence spending, presenting it as necessary to peace, order and, by extension, development. At

71

the same time we must be wary of the trap in which it is believed that, could we but persuade the super powers to disarm, an immediate millennium of universal development would ensue. To begin with, there is no guarantee that resources released by reductions in arms expenditure would be diverted to support Third World development. Furthermore, the dilemma of development is not restricted to the question of aid flows from North to South. That dilemma is buried in the structural relations between North and South. Hence, we must approach the subject of development by recognising the existing political realities, the entrenched interests, and the immutable defence ideologies which exist.

For political action, aimed at the objectives of disarmament and development, to be effectively focussed, it is necessary to analyse the historical forces at work on each objective process, both together and separately. Only then can we hope to consider how these two objectives, each an imperative of our times, might be pursued in a mutually reinforcing manner.

Complex Triad

The history of the world since 1945 has been shaped by three major impulses. The *first* has been created by the emergence of the United States as the dominant power of the world capitalist system with its concomitant status as leader of the so-called "free" world. The critical factor in this process has been the rapid expansion of US productive capacity during World War II, leaving its capital poised for the take-off into world dominance as soon as that war came to an end. However, even as US power was taking its quantum leap forward, the Soviet Union was acting to establish its own hegemony in Eastern Europe.

As the USA financed the revitalisation of the Western

economic system with the Marshall Plan, its military establishment became intoxicated with all that was implied by sole possession of the atom bomb. General Maxwell Taylor wrote that the bomb would allow the US "to police the world through the threat of its use". Moving from the general to the particular, US Army General Mitchell wrote, "the old theory that victory means destruction of the hostile main army is untenable . . . It is now realised that the hostile main army in the field is a false objective. . . Armies themselves can be disregarded if a rapid strike is made against the opposing centres." Thus was born the "Nuclear Theology" with its notions of the pre-emptive strike, the first strike and the preventative war. It is to these beginnings that we trace the longest of the shadows under which modern man must live.

In the meantime, the Soviet Union, which had emerged from World War II with huge conventional land forces, awoke to the fact that these were meaningless in the face of the atomic bomb and the rockets which were soon available to deliver it. The story of how the Soviet Union developed its own atomic and rocket capability; of the resulting nuclear stand-off; of the paradox that nuclear parity restores the importance of conventional forces; of the system of alliances such as the North Atlantic Treaty Organisation (NATO) and the South-East Asia treaty on the one hand and the Warsaw Pact on the other; of the culmination of all these processes in the present expenditure of one trillion dollars annually, involves a history as familiar as it is tragic.

Even as the USA and the Soviet Union have pursued the path of their own dialectical inter-reaction, the *second* great impulse of contemporary history has been unfolding. Beginning in the year 1947 in India, the decolonisation process has swept through Asia, the Middle East, Africa and the Caribbean. More than a hundred new nations have claimed and won their independence as the political structures of the great empires of the sixteenth to nineteenth centuries have yielded to new impulses towards freedom. However, the new nations have been without exception, creations of the economic forces which first established the Mercantilist System and later pressed more than half of the globe into the service of the Industrial Revolution.

Within a generation of India's independence, one half of the world's population was discovering that its new political freedom did not alter the economic facts of life. The colonial world had been assigned a place in the international division of labour. It was a place at the bottom, and subject to laws of unequal exchange. The control of capital and technology at the centres of economic power added an element of inexorable exploitation to relationships that were inherently unequal. Furthermore, colonialism and its companion, economic imperialism, had created economies locked in relationships that are politely described as interdependent. However, they are more realistically understood to be dependencies that arise strictly from and through the control of capital and technology.

The *third* major impulse of modern history has been created by the search for systems of international management. At the economic level, the Bretton Woods Agreement of 1944 was made by forty-four nations and created the International Monetary Fund (IMF) and the World Bank as key elements in a system designed to avoid the catastrophic failure of the capitalist system and to manage its international relations in the 1920s and 1930s. Concomitantly, the United Nations was created as part of a search for a new system of collective security.

Bretton Woods demonstrated a maturing within the capitalist system. The new arrangements were designed to ensure a stable climate for an economic system which had superseded national boundaries and could no longer afford irrational national behaviour. However, these arrangements did not contemplate the emergence of the Third World and were not designed to cope with the problems of development which the Third World is required to face. Meantime, the UN could be seen as a reaction to the implications of global conflict. However, the retention of the veto power by the major countries which won World War II is decisive evidence that the nation state with its notions of sovereignty and right to self-serving, independent action is not ready to yield its power to any form of international institution.

Interaction

The interaction between the forces leading to super-power rivalry, the struggle for Third World development and the post-war multilateral institutions is complex but always concrete.

From the outset the dialogue in the UN system has led to a general acceptance of the value of overseas development assistance from the developed to the developing nations. This has been variously justified as morally desirable; as a means of redress following centuries of colonial exploitation; or as a pre-condition of general economic growth from which developed and developing nations would benefit alike. The funds made available to the World Bank and the IMF for disbursement under carefully regulated conditions to developing countries can be said to reflect this same impulse. On the other hand, the scale on which these funds are made available has been historically proven to be unequal to the task of Third World development, however modestly defined. Many are the voices that have called for more aid and more sympathetic IMF policies, but to no effect. Indeed, to understand why the promptings of morality and common sense have proven unavailing, one must examine the other elements in the equation.

The reason development assistance has been inadequate is twofold. As the East/West conflict has intensified, national budgets have been increasingly devoted to military expenditure. Simultaneously, the system of unequal exchange in which the Third World is trapped has required levels of capital formation and types of development strategy undreamed of at the beginning of the decolonisation process. Thus, one of the major factors, the East-West conflict, has actively militated against the possibility of Third World development; a second decolonisation has served mainly to reveal the real proportions of the problem, making it clear that aid must be accompanied by restructuring.

Since 1974 the interaction has become both more complex and more debilitating. The Vietnam War was pursued in all its gruesome futility because of a perception that the East/West conflict was about to take on a North/South dimension. At the same time, the huge military expenditure of that war fuelled international inflation to levels which the economic system could not contain. As prices began to soar the Organization of Petroleum Exporting Countries (OPEC) counter-attacked by increasing oil prices. The ultimate victims of this vicious circle were the non-oil-exporting developing countries. Faced with the problem of acute shortages of foreign exchange they began to borrow from the commercial banking system. Most petro-dollars flowed back to Western banks which now proceeded to onlend the money on increasingly stringent terms to the very countries that were most in trouble and had the least capacity to defend themselves. The debt crisis resulted directly from this interaction between the East-West conflict and the weakness of Third World economic structures. But that was not the end of the process.

As Third World countries sank deeply into debt, they were forced to turn to the IMF. This institution was not concerned with development, its primary purpose being to apply corrective measures to secure the repayment of the loans which the commercial banks had made. Thus, the principal institution of Bretton Woods, which had been created to facilitate the growth of trade by stabilising economic relationships, now became the main enforcer of the commercial banking system. To ensure that money would be available to repay the loans, the IMF compelled scores of developing nations to slash expenditures on social services; restrict wages; and implement massive devaluations which put marginal populations to the sword of hunger.

The resulting contraction of internal demand had two horrifying results. In the first place, these arrangements served to slow down internal economic activity. Then again, in a direct social consequence they severely reduced living standards. The interaction between these two factors led to growing social unrest and political instability. As the night follows the day, instability was followed in many Third World countries by increasing military expenditure as governments sought to contain what they perceived as "trouble".

By now the dialectical process had assumed macabre proportions. The perception of Third World instability led many US strategic thinkers to press for increased military strength in the West as a hedge against the danger of the spread of Communism to the Third World. In 1976 President Carter pledged a 3% increase in military expenditure, an ambition rendered modest in the extreme by the subsequent increase of the Reagan administration. In due course, the Soviet Union was compounding the difficulties by adding the SS-20 missile to the European atomic confrontation. At the same time, it invaded Afghanistan in response to its fears of Islamic fundamentalism, which many see as an expression of the stresses experienced by Third World communities. Adding its own dimension to the general insanity is the increasing, and of course, uni-directional flow of arms from the North, West and East, to an increasingly unstable Third World or South.

In 1987, Third World debt stood at $1,000 billion. It strangles growth and inhibits world trade. Developing countries slash education, health services and essential imports as they contract internal and external expenditure to meet interest charges. Each year a country like Jamaica must spend nearly half of every foreign exchange dollar earned to keep up with its obligations. In 1986 Peru owed more for that year than its gross earnings, forcing President Alan Garcia to act decisively. Mozambique has been destabilised by South Africa to the extent that one full year's earnings of foreign exchange cannot pay the interest on its debt. Repayments of principal do not even arise. Brazil is now in the throes of a similar crisis. Sub-Saharan Africa simply cannot pay, nor can it hope to do so in this century. Indeed, so great are the debt-servicing charges and so severe the reduction of capital flows, that there has been a reverse flow of resources from South to North of $125 billion over the last four years. At the same time, arms expenditure at $1,000 billion annually pre-empts resources which are desperately needed for development. The social consequences are cruel. Even more cruel is the fact that there is no path to growth where survival itself is in doubt.

In the midst of the encircling gloom we must nevertheless ask ourselves whether there are any positive signs. In particular, we must consider the implications of the various negotiations aimed at arms control. The Strategic Arms Limitation Treaty (SALT) of 1977 flattered to deceive in the sense that it led to no fundamental alteration in the equations of the East/West confrontation. Nor did it herald any new approach to the world economy and the place of the Third World in it. It was an arrangement of convenience between two powers for whom the opportunity costs of further strategic arms expenditure had subsided temporarily to zero.

By the same token, the various periods of reduced tension which we describe as "detente" do not reflect basic changes in strategic thinking. Rather, they are like those moments when a pair of boxers circle each other to catch their breath, waiting for a new surge of energy. The real indicators which we must examine for new thinking lie in attitudes towards the world economic system and its structural defects in commodity trading; untrammelled power at the disposal of trans-national corporations; and the chronic haemorrhage of wealth from South to North through the terms of trade and debt servicing. Yet with the world economy severely handicapped by the debt crisis, and millions starving for want of indigenous agricultural development, there is not even a willingness to hold an international conference to tackle these crises in the human condition. Arms control, maybe! Debt relief, never!

Is there a basis for hope?

In 1947, Walter Lippmann popularised the term "Cold War". However, the originator of the phrase was the fourteenth century Spanish writer, Don Juan Mañuel, who, commenting on the conflict between Christians and Muslims at the time, remarked, "war that is very strong and very hot ends either with death or peace, whereas cold war neither brings peace nor gives honour to the one who makes it". It is in this context that one takes note of developments in the Soviet Union since the accession to office of Mikhail Gorbachev.

For forty years East/West relations got no further than the notion of peaceful co-existence between two economic and political systems. However, the inarticulate major premise upon which this doctrine was based, was the assumption that co-existence was a tactical pause until some unspecified time when one system or the other would prevail, due to its inherent superiority. Now, for the first time, Gorbachev has introduced, at the least, a rhetoric of respect in which historical validity is conceded to the other side. He speaks also of the reality that disarmament cannot precede but must be the consequence of a system of security in which all parties believe. This critical implication of *glasnost* for international relations deserves to be explored. But this can only happen if a parallel gesture is made by the West, conceding historical validity to the Soviet Union. Neither is likely in the conditions of the "Cold War". But both are possible if they are pursued simultaneously by strong leadership with a commitment to new possibilities. If disarmament is to occur and general development to be pursued as a common human enterprise, a start must be made in the redefinition of social responsibility, according to it an international dimension. The question is whether this represents an idealist fantasy.

Let us examine history for pointers. If we begin with the nation-state, we can distinguish three clear processes. Firstly, economic formations demand the creation of strong, central political authority if they are to proceed to their logical fulfilment. The existence of the authority facilitates economic development but comes increasingly under pressure to adjust the more harmful social consequences of the economic process. Secondly, and in response to these pressures, doctrines of social responsibility are developed to justify the use of political power in the interest of social regulation. Thirdly, in the end, the political process becomes the arena in which economic development and social benefit are optimised.

The economic outreach of the nation-state has now created a parallel international process. It has become commonplace in discusssion of today's world to assert that we have become interdependent. Phrases like "global village" may be fanciful; and certainly interdependence does not always describe equal relationships. On the other hand, the forces of production, distribution and communication have created a new reality of interconnectedness in an irreversible process. There is a sense, therefore, in which the new economic formations which span national boundaries are beginning to demand adjustments to political arrangements as we know them. Sooner or later the forces of production are going to require a capacity within the political systems of the world to facilitate their fulfilment. This does not imply world government. On the other hand, it does imply a recognition that political systems will have to be modified in ways that facilitate the globalisation of economic activity. All economic logic cries out for trade and exchange between East and West. Equally, economic logic cries out for both institutions and resources to eliminate the debt crisis. And, most of all, economic sanity demands a general system of management: of commodity trading, accountability for trans-national corporations and measures to facilitate capital flows to the mutual advantage of North and South.

The multilateral system which was put in place after World War II could, and still can, provide the starting point for wise and equitable management of the world economy. Unhappily, multilateralism is now under siege. Led by the USA and to a lesser extent the UK, the institutions of the UN are under either direct attack or threat.

Charles Maynes, the editor of *Foreign Policy* has written recently on US-Third World policy and the US approach to international institutions. On Third World policy he observes "the Reagan Administration has consistently stressed instruments of force in its policy towards the Third World. Total US foreign aid nearly doubled between 1981 and 1985 to reach a level of $19.2 billion. But the portion of the aid budget devoted to security concerns rose from roughly half of the fiscal year (FY) 1981 foreign-aid budget to more than two-thirds of the FY 1985 budget. The administration plans to raise this portion further, to more than 70%, by FY 1988. The administration has used military force in Grenada and Lebanon and against Libya. It has threatened the use of military force against Iran, Nicaragua and Syria. It has conducted menacing military manoeuvres near Cuba and Nicaragua."

On international institutions Charles Maynes recounts with telling force the accumulation of policies aimed at the rolling-back of multilateralism. "The Administration has withdrawn from UNESCO (United Nations Educational Scientific and Cultural Organisation) and declared it will no longer follow a policy of automatic compliance with the decisions of the International Court of Justice. It has threatened to withdraw from the Food and Agricultural Organisation, the International Atomic Energy Agency and the UN Conference on Trade and Development. It had repudiated the earlier understanding among major donors that the seventh replenishment of funds for the World Bank's International Development Association would be at a level at least equal in real terms to that of the last replenishment. By limiting the US contribution to no more than $2.25 billion over three years, the Administration has forced a 40% cut in real terms in the Bank's funds for soft loans. The Administration has refused to sign the Law of the Sea Treaty laboriously negotiated on a bipartisan basis over the course of four Administrations. It has refused to continue contributions to the UN Fund for Population Activities, and it cast the lone vote against a World Health Organisation code of conduct regarding the manufacture and distribution of infant milk formula. Furthermore, it is the first Administration in post-war history to fail to defend international institutions against congressional pressures, which have now resulted in the Kassebaum Amendment that unilaterally reduces the mandated US contribution to the United Nations from 25% of the budget to 20% unless the General Assembly adopts a form of weighted voting on financial issues – a step that requires amendement of the UN Charter. Even more extreme measures seem likely to pass through the congress this year."

The Extent of Waste

The agenda for peace and equitable development is consistent with the logic of history. But, as we can see, the action that needs to be taken runs counter to the grain of events. Not the least of the problems is the huge apparatus of production and the scale of profits which depend on the arms industry. *Fortune* magazine showed recently that the average percentage return to investors in the ten years from 1974–84 for the largest 500 corporations was 18.65%. Amongst aero-space and armament corporations this figure was 26.76%.

Then, there is the link between finance capital and the armaments industry. In 1985 financial institutions held 75% of the shares of Lockheed and 55% of Rockwell International, to give but two examples.

However, all this may well fade into insignificance beside the Star Wars programme. Beginning with a modest appropriation of $1 billion in 1984, expenditure is scheduled to rise to $7.3 billion in 1989. *Time* magazine, which is not noted for its leadership in the peace movement, went straight to the heart of the matter recently when it stated, "The Administration calls the program the Strategic Defence Initiative, the press has dubbed it 'Star Wars', and the hundreds of companies and universities competing to work on the project could easily rename it 'Star Bucks'." Experts estimate that the Star Wars programme could ultimately cost anywhere from $400 billion to $1.2 trillion. It could thus become the biggest bonanza ever for American business and educational institutes.

Even now, the possibility of an agreement on intermediate- and short-range missiles must be set against the call by the US Administration for new funds for Star Wars. To see these figures in context, one may set them against five statistics:

1. 25 million people have died in conflicts since 1945;
2. Infant mortality rates in areas of the Third World are equal to those of Europe in 1570;
3. There is one soldier for every 43 people, yet only one doctor for every 1,030 people.
4. The estimated cost of a modern long-range bomber is $200 million. 17 bombers are roughly equal to the total expenditure on health in sub-Saharan Africa;
5. Six percent of the world military budget of 1984 would be sufficient to double the amount of official development assistance to developing nations.

Parts of the Third World are also guilty and cannot be absolved from their role in global militarisation. Indeed, the Third World's share of global military expenditure has increased from less than 4% in 1955 to over 15% in the 1980s. Arms exports from the North to the South have accounted for a substantial share of the world's arms trade. Military expenditure in developing countries, especially in the Middle East, consumes an unacceptably large share of GDP given the desperately low standard of living of the majority of people. In Latin America between 1972 and 1982, per capita income grew by 1.6 % while military expenditure grew by 6% and overall arms purchases by 13.2%. Indeed, it has been estimated that in the last ten years, 20% of all new loans were raised to buy arms.

Then there has been the case of the OPEC countries.

Writing in the *World Policy Journal*, Altaf Gauhar, the editor of *South Magazine*, has described the uses to which oil revenues were put. He says "guns were the first claimants. The explosion in oil revenues produced parallel explosions in military spending. The price of oil increased fourfold in 1974 and arms expenditures among Arab producers showed a corresponding increase between 1974 and 1976. Oil prices doubled in 1980, as did arms expenditures between 1980 and 1984. Kuwait's annual military expenditures were less than $200 million before 1974. After the oil price increase in 1974, they shot up to over $1 billion in 1975 and to $1.6 billion in 1982. Saudi Arabia spent a little over $9 billion on defense in 1976. By 1981, that figure had risen to $22 billion. In less than 20 years military expenditures in the Middle East escalated from $4.7 billion in 1962 to $46.7 billion. In 1980, nearly nine times the world average."

Later in the same article he states, "while the oil bonanza spurred an explosion in military spending, the current decline in oil revenues has not resulted in any reduction in arms expenditures. In some instances, military budgets have even gone up. In the United Arab Emirates, when oil revenues declined from $19 billion in 1980 to $13 billion in 1983, half of the federal budget of $6 billion in 1982 was still spent on defense; in 1983 this increased to 60 per cent while severe cutbacks were being made in the social sector. Salaries for primary and secondary school teachers were not paid in time and scores of teachers were laid off in 1983 and 1984, but there was no abatement in military expenditure".

Now this military expenditure in the Third World can only be understood if it is situated within the context of the economic and political structures of the world economy. The poverty and under-development in the South is largely due to the historical experience, the structural distortions, institutional inadequacies and the role assigned to it in the international division of labour. I make this point because most of the exercising of military power, and therefore the motivation for military expenditure, is accounted for by internal repression rather than defence against external threats. It is only development which will reduce the economic deprivations that spawn the intense social tensions which often manifest themselves in violent political confrontations. The efforts towards development and disarmament must be pursued within the South both collectively and within individual nation-states, but cannot be meaningfully separated from an accompanying global economic reform.

Clearly, the logic of history has to contend with formidable obstacles and deeply entrenched vested interests. It is the same forces which escalate the East-West confrontations; seek the militarisation of space; erode the multilateral institutions; reject an international conference on debt; refuse to discuss the restructuring of the global economy; and increasingly insist on ideological conformity as the precondition of co-operation. Nonetheless, I refuse to succumb to despair. The stakes are too high when we consider the immense possibilities for advances in general welfare which are put within our reach by science, technology and productive capability; or for an end to civilisation as we know it.

Of course, many in the North argue that the South is powerless and may be safely ignored. Yet it might pause to remember that a quarter of its current growth rate of 3% is due to the lower price of commodities, including oil, from the South. Can it really ignore permanently so significant a contributor to its own hopes for success?

Some of the answers to all this are going to be provided by the South itself as it is driven to explore its own options in collective self-reliance. But the South cannot do it alone; nor does it suit the North to turn its back. Indeed, the evolution of a new politics of international co-operation aimed at equitable development opportuni-

ties within the global economy is the over-riding imperative of our times. The thrust towards such a movement
must begin unapologetically with a moral view of society
and the individual, and of the relations between societies.
Thereafter we must identify a specific agenda to be
pursued relentlessly at all levels of the political process,
an agenda which unites the positive elements in the
political systems of East and West and of North and
South. At least four items in such an agenda suggest
themselves.

1. *East/West*

Firstly, we must identify the steps which need to be
taken to create an effective system of collective security. Specific initiatives like the "Zero Option" and
more general programmes of phased disarmament must
be understood to be the objective of a system of
collective security once it is in place. Even the prospect
of an early agreement to eliminate nuclear weapons
from Europe will prove misleading unless it is treated
as a point of departure for a more fundamental exercise.
At the same time, some of the funds saved must be
earmarked for a general compliance with the UN target
of 0.7% of GDP for official development assistance.

Secondly, we need a decision by the Soviet-linked
COMECON countries to become fully involved in both
the discussion of and the decisions concerning the
management and restructuring of the world economy.

2. *North/North*

A programme of general, internationally planned reflation by the major industrial economies is the necessary
precursor to a new era of economic expansion which
can exercise a powerful "pull effect" among the economies of developing countries. If this reflation is carried
out simultaneously by a number of like-minded governments of the North, it can stimulate substantial
growth, put millions of workers in the North back on

the job and, by increasing trade, reduce unit costs of production and offset the danger of inflation. The increased activity will affect the demand for the commodities of the South and make room in the markets of the North for the new manufacturing industries of the South.

3. *North/South*

An international conference on debt is an urgent priority. The objective of such a conference would be to substantially reduce the proportion of foreign exchange earnings which developing economies must now devote to the servicing of debt. This can be accomplished by imaginative techniques such as an internationally backed debt bond of high security but with long maturities and low interest rates. These can be used to replace the high yielding loans which the commercial banks can no longer collect, producing the simultaneous benefit of security in the banks' loan portfolio with manageable levels of payments for Third World countries. Existing multilateral institutions such as the IMF can arrange and supervise appropriate conditionalities to ensure the prudent management and development orientation of the resources which would be released by such a programme.

A resolution of the debt crisis should be a prelude to re-opening the dialogue on the world economy. Priorities to be examined should include new levels of resources at the disposal of the multilateral institutions to ensure that stabilisation programmes are followed by actual growth; a system of management of world commodity trade to provide stability to prices along with measures to offset the chronic deterioration in the terms of trade; reform of the monetary system; the elimination of protectionism and the expansion of free trade; a code of conduct for trans-national corporations.

4. *South/South*

First, we must begin with intense study of development strategies throughout the countries of the South with particular regard to the types and levels of political mobilisation which are necessary to support local capital formation in the context of self-reliance. The South must also study the phasing of social benefits so that social advances are sufficiently real to maintain faith and sustain hope; but not implemented with a recklessness that undermines the capacity for self-sustaining economic growth.

Secondly, there should be a relentless pursuit by the South of collective self-reliance through programmes of South/South co-operation in production, trade and research.

Thirdly, there must be efforts to create collective security arrangements among countries of the South, in particular on a regional basis. This would permit a reduction of military expenditure in the name of defence from external threat. The savings may be substantial, for example, in areas like naval surveillance.

This will all call for a new consensus in the North between the progressive parties, progressive elements in nominally conservative parties, the intellectuals, the trade unions and the far-sighted entrepreneurs and financiers.

It demands no less unprecedented political action throughout the countries of the South. Every institution which provides links across national boundaries, through which these issues can be discussed, must be exploited patiently and tirelessly in the search for a consensus among all patriotic groups. The South in particular cannot afford the luxury of the narrow nationalism in which suspicions thrive, latent hostilities fester and strategic co-operation languishes.

The forces of the status quo have no need for organisation. Fear and self interest can take care of their agenda! By contrast, the possibilities of the future can be demonstrated by common sense, but rest upon no evidential basis. They must, therefore, be the object of ceaseless mobilisation. It is to that task that we are summoned by our despair in the present no less than by our hopes for the future.

The Arms Race and Poverty

JOAN RUDDOCK
with PETER CRAMPTON

Joan Ruddock was elected to Parliament as Labour MP for Lewisham–Deptford in June 1987. In Parliament she has pursued her interest in foreign affairs, alongside the demanding work of representing an inner-city constituency. She is Vice-Chair of the backbench departmental defence committee, a member of the Council of Europe and of the Western European Union.

Joan Ruddock was educated at Imperial College, London University. In 1981 she became the national Chairperson of the Campaign for Nuclear Disarmament, a post she held until 1984. She has travelled the world speaking for CND, including a speech on behalf of non-governmental organisations to the United Nations in 1982. She has led a number of delegations to the Soviet Union and one to China.

In 1984 she was awarded the Frank Cousins Peace Prize by the Transport and General Workers' Union.

Joan Ruddock has been active in anti-racist campaigns and a member of the Anti-Apartheid Movement since student days. She is a founder member of One World.

> The arms race pre-empts resources that
> might be used more productively to dimin-
> ish security threats created by environmen-
> tal conflicts and the resentments that are
> fuelled by widespread poverty. ("Our
> Common Future", Report of World Com-
> mission on Environment and Development,
> 1987)

> It would be a contradiction in terms to rely
> for . . . disarmament, on the actions of those
> who manage and benefit from the interna-
> tional military order. They are part of the
> problem which the disarmament move-
> ments set out to solve. (*Economics of Mili-
> tarism* by D. and R. Smith, Pluto Press,
> 1983)

The global military build-up since 1945 is without precedent in the world's history. At its core is the Cold War
and the massive military expenditures of the USA and
the USSR. But the arms race has spread far beyond the
super powers.

In Britain public debate has centred on nuclear
weapons. Nuclear weapons have also been the main focus
of arms control and, more recently, arms reduction talks
between the super powers. But, while these weapons are

crucial to the process of militarisation, they are not the principal users of resources.

Overall, the arms race consumes a vast amount of the world's riches. It diverts the skills of large numbers of people to devising more efficient killing machines and it has led to the militarisation of societies with a consequent erosion of civil liberties. The arms race also distorts national economies and the world's economic system; even the United States has severe difficulties with huge budget and trade deficits. But the economic effects are at their worst in the Third World. While the military almost everywhere is able to obtain most of the resources it wants, the majority of the people of this world live in poverty. In Third World societies, dominated by the military, the problem is not just that money is spent on weapons; it is often the military who are the best housed, clothed and fed – and the military are, of course, predominately men. Producing food, carrying fuel and water and looking after children is women's work and there is no doubt that world priorities which place the arms race so high and basic needs so low, also place women in an inferior and exploited position.

Clearly, if resources were transferred from the military to development, with the aid of modern technology and political will most of the problems of poverty could be solved. But the processes of disarmament and development are more subtly linked, and these links are no new discovery. United Nations reports have defined them over many years – the General Assembly having adopted thirty-one resolutions referring specifically to the misallocation of resources by governments. With very few exceptions, governments have failed to put into practice what they have endorsed publicly at the United Nations.

While a sudden switch of resources from the military to development is not realistic, practical goals ought to be established and could be achieved. Only when there is hope of change is change likely.

The Arms Race

Ruth Sivard's *World, Military and Social Expenditures* (*World Priorities*, USA, 1987) records the progress of the arms race. In 1984 military expenditure worldwide totalled US $752 billion. By 1987 it had risen – officially – to US $846 billion. But many experts believe it is more like US $1,000 billion. This represents 5.6% of world gross national product (GNP) or about US $30,000 spent for every soldier on the planet.

This contrasts with 4.9% spent on education and 4.1% on health. There is one soldier for every forty-three people, yet only one doctor for every 1,030 people. Every minute US $2½ million is spent on the military, and every minute thirty children die from hunger and preventable disease, and while US $200 per head each year is spent on the arms race, a mere 6 cents is devoted to international peace-keeping work.

Military expenditure is not evenly spread – the two super powers account for 58%, (or nearly 75% if all North Atlantic Treaty Organization (NATO) and Warsaw Treaty Organisation (WTO) countries are included). Spending by the developing world has dramatically increased in recent years, rising from 8% in 1960 to 20% in 1985.

Such vast amounts of money could make a major impact on human suffering if redirected and even small amounts could do much. For example, the World Health Organization's projected malaria eradication campaign would cost about US $8 billion – three days' military expenditure. Malaria kills one million people a year. Measles kills nearly two million children each year, yet it could be eradicated for the cost of five hours of world military spending or half an "attack" submarine.

Security

All state authorities justify military spending on the grounds of national security, which raises the most fundamental question – what is security?

For the individual, while security obviously includes freedom from the threat of aggression to the state, it also must include access to basic resources for a fulfilling life – food, clothing, shelter, health, education. Individual security also means freedom from state repression.

The nation state seeks national security either alone or through alliances. This is the traditional interpretation of security borne out in a joint submission of the European Community states to a United Nations conference in 1987: "Emphasis is rightly put on the enormous volume of military spending needed to provide a degree of security that in many cases is still too fragile." Throughout the report, security is identified exclusively with military power and as a situation sought by one nation or bloc without reference to the rest of the world.

This view of security means that individuals are subsumed into the general concept of the state, and while the state may devote enormous resources to protecting itself against external threat, the people comprising that state may be suffering insecurity of a very high order. The question must be asked of NATO – are the people of Western Europe more secure now than they were in the past? Opinions vary, but the constant escalation in military spending has failed to achieve lasting security and other approaches ought to be considered.

Yet the responses of military men remain outdated, and Cold-War-type thinking still pervades present-day military decisions. In Europe, both NATO and the WTO have long since integrated nuclear weapons into their conventional war-fighting strategies. These nuclear battle-field tactics would destroy those they were supposedly designed to protect. Individual security has been sacrificed for "national security", based on the now discredited theory of nuclear deterrence. In seeking an unattainable goal, both blocs have failed to realise an essential truth of the modern, nuclear age – that the West can only be secure if the East is secure and vice versa – in other words, common security is essential. The problem of security thus becomes a political one to be solved by political means.

Meanwhile, the arms race itself has become a threat to security. In many respects, the race is technological, usually led by the United States, and based on the illusion that there is always a technical solution to a political problem. Star Wars, with its supposedly impenetrable shield over the USA, is but the latest attempt. The pursuit of *all* technologies to increase the killing power of conventional weapons is another example. Conventional wars, involving sophisticated weapons, have proliferated, especially in the Third World. The distinction between combatants and non-combatants has become non-existent, so the civilian death toll has risen, both in wars and, in the South, in the almost inevitable famines caused by them.

Security at all levels is threatened by another characteristic of the current arms race – dominance abroad. Three quarters of the 2 million troops based outside their national territories are from the super powers. This requires military bases abroad, many in the developing world.

Dominance is also shown in the readiness of both super powers to intervene in conflicts where they consider their interests might be threatened. Intervention can be direct as in Vietnam, Afghanistan, Grenada or Libya, or indirect, with proxies and arms sales being the chief methods. National security as "territorial integrity" takes on a new meaning when the whole world is viewed as a legitimate area of national interest.

All the evidence indicates that the world is increasingly

a less secure place and that, as Caroline Thomas says in her book *In Search of Security: the Third World in International Relations, 1987* "Ultimately, security is not the product of the fulfilment of a particular military equation, neither can it be regarded as a national problem." The drive for security through the expansion of military force has failed, and in failure millions have been killed and many more made homeless, hungry and destitute. Clearly what is needed is an alternative system of international relations where military strength is no longer the sole arbiter.

There are many non-military threats to security which require co-operation and compromise and cannot be solved by confrontation. They include those associated with the world economic crisis – unemployment, inflation, the debt burden, international trade and monetary instability. These problems are compounded in the developing world by the strict conditions frequently imposed on debtor nations by the International Monetary Fund, by the production and marketing policies of many multinational companies and by the farming support systems of the industrial world.

Such problems represent real threats to people's security. The Kenyan woman trying to grow millet on barren land is more concerned about the irrigated fields of carnations nearby than the nuclear weapons of the super powers. Ethiopia was exporting large amounts of vegetables to Europe when the 1984 famine was at its height.

Security must be viewed in a much wider sense than military force. It must take into account security of food supplies, health, education, the economy and trading systems – thus development and security are linked.

A wider definition of security makes the need for a new system of managing the global economy very clear. Such a system would recognise that the economic dominance of multinational companies and the political dominance of the bloc system are barriers to development. It would elevate the importance of international fora where rich and poor countries could sit down together to discuss problems of security. It would demand full participation in the United Nations and its agencies, acceptance of decisions by the International Court and the implementation of decisions of international bodies, even if they conflict with narrow national interests. Common security for a common future is incompatible with the global arms race.

The Impact of Militarisation

THE ENVIRONMENT

The whole planet is affected by environmental problems whose importance is only just beginning to be publicly realised. The deterioration in the environment is clearly a threat to all – individuals, nations and the planet itself, but particularly to future generations. As the Brundtland Report says, "Most of today's decision-makers will be dead before the planet suffers the full consequences of acid rain, global warming, ozone depletion, widespread desertification and species loss. Most of today's young voters will be alive." Many would add the results of the development of nuclear technology to the list, for, even without considering the effects of nuclear weapons, the problems associated with nuclear waste and the release of radioactivity into the environment are still only just coming to light.

Varying degrees of environmental damage are related to the arms race. In the most extreme cases, in the Pacific, parts of the environment have been completely destroyed by nuclear testing and many islands to which populations have been forcibly removed, are severely affected by radio-activity. At a less extreme level, nuclear establishments in Britain are surrounded by clusters of cancers affecting children in particular. In more general terms, environmental stress can be seen to be both a cause and an effect of political tension and military conflict. This has been demonstrated most clearly in recent years in the Horn of Africa (Ethiopia/Eritrea/Somalia) where disasters, though exacerbated by natural forces, have all too frequently been man-made.

THE ARMS RACE AND INDUSTRIAL SOCIETIES

The political forces at work in the industrial world since 1945 have led to a situation which has been described by Dan Smith in *Economics of Militarism* as "institutionalised permanent military confrontation". Hopefully the agreement on intermediate nuclear forces between the super powers in December 1987 may have blunted this military confrontation a little, but as yet the basic pattern remains unchanged. Two blocs of previously undreamt-of military power still confront each other globally – and hold the rest of the world and their own citizens hostage.

At a general level, the arms race and development both call on resources which at any one time are finite. But they do not compete equally. Given that military confrontation between the super powers and their allies is thought to have become permanent and that the power structures in the industrial world accept a very limited idea of security, they cannot compete equally.

Thus even in "mature" democracies, the allocation of resources becomes one-sided. Militarised parts of society become over powerful: they identify the "threat"; they judge the appropriate response; and they control the decision-making. So one of the main political effects of the arms race, especially where nuclear weapons are concerned, is a restriction of democracy.

Britain is a very instructive example, as the Oxford Research Group has demonstrated: "Parliament knows nothing of decisions (on nuclear weapons and many other military expenditures) until the government decides to tell it" and while the Ministry of Defence does not have to consult the Foreign and Commonwealth Office on matters in the field of foreign policy, the FCO must consult the MOD on all issues concerning defence. If defence against external threats was made subordinate to and dependent on international relations policy then the military would have less control. And if the whole area of defence- and security-spending were opened up to public scrutiny there would be greater accountability. Instead, the British Government confines the first acts of decision-taking in any programme to a few non-elected officials, maintains secrecy from the elected representatives and the public generally, and has a secret service that is willing to be used in a partial manner for political ends.

Military spending also has an economic impact quite the opposite of that often claimed for it. In fact the military sector is not a great provider of jobs; military spending is one of the least efficient kinds of public spending in job-creation terms. Furthermore it drains away funds that could relieve poverty and distress. The very nature of military spending heightens tensions, reduces security and sustains the system which makes even more arms necessary.

High levels of military spending are associated with low growth rates in productivity, both because of the constraints they create in the civilian sector of the economy and because they do not add to the capital stock for future production. Defence industries have a lower potential for creating employment because they are so capital intensive. Recent experience in Britain proves that even with a rising military budget employment in modern weapons factories falls. Furthermore, in Britain 54% of all government funding on research goes to military projects and one third of all scientists and technologists work in the defence area.

Yet, after a United Nations General Assembly resolution in 1982 urging all governments to make national studies in preparation for conversion from military to peaceful production, only the Swedish Government responded. However, several studies have been carried out by trade unions in Britain and the United States. There are no serious technical or economic difficulties, but conversion must be planned for. Practical plans would also increase confidence in the sincerity to go through with negotiations and so, of themselves, would reduce tension.

The Arms Race and the Developing World

Whether the already rich countries have the right to spend so much on the arms race is debatable. However, it is a fact that by their arms spending the countries of the North do have powerful indirect effects on the lives of those in developing countries. There are also direct effects on the South stemming from its relationship to the North. The arms trade and the debt burden are two of these.

THE ARMS TRADE

Companies and governments in the industrial world want to defray some of their huge military costs, so they encourage arms exports. The value of this trade is over US $300 billion worldwide, of which 66% is earned by the United States and the Soviet Union and a further 20% by France, Britain, West Germany, Czechoslovakia, Italy and China. These states export mainly to countries in their 'bloc' and to those they are seeking to influence for a variety of purposes − trade, acquisition of bases, protection of perceived national economic or political interests ... The suppliers of arms can change: Ethiopia originally received arms from the United States and its allies; now it receives them from the Soviet Union.

Countries in the same alliance often supply opposing sides – as when Britain sold arms to Nigeria while France supplied Biafra, during the Biafran War. In the Falklands' War British ships were sunk with French weapons and British weapons are being used by both Iran and Iraq in the Gulf. Hypocrisy abounds, as when John Birch (the UK representative) told a UN conference in 1987 that developing countries spent too much on arms!

Global arms trading continues to expand, and countries wanting weapons can always find a ready supplier, but there has been a decline of imports into many Third World countries, especially in Africa. This is, in large part, due to the worldwide economic crisis and particularly the debt problem, but also because some developing countries now have considerable arms industries of their own – Brazil, for example, is now an exporter.

Over three quarters of arms imports go to countries where many, if not most, of the people lack even the basic necessities of life. Britain has sold over a hundred Hawk fighters to such countries, each sale representing the resources for a clean water supply for one and a half million people. There is a shared responsibility between rich and poor countries. Even without the most destructive weapons wars in the Third World are catastrophic because of the death and disruption in societies where life is already so close to the margins of existence.

THE ARMS RACE AND THE DEBT PROBLEM

The arms race, particularly the super power nuclear build-up, has directly affected the debt burden. Developing countries were encouraged to take out large loans, at low but variable interest rates, in the period after the oil price increases of the early 1970s. In the late 1970s the USA embarked on a succession of very expensive military programmes – cruise missiles, MX, Pershing, B1 bomber, Trident submarines and finally, most expensive of all, SDI. In 1987 the American military budget was about

$280 billion – a 25% increase in just four years. This was largely financed by budget deficits, which drew in money from outside attracted by high interest rates. In 1985 US $150 billion of West European capital (that could have financed much needed industrial investment) went to the USA. But much more serious has been the increasing net transfer of money from the debtor developing countries, which by 1985 had reached $74 billion. Even the IMF has said, "The United States is solving its problems at other people's expense, importing capital that weaker countries need for their development."

Surely something is radically wrong with an international system where the poorest people finance weapons programmes, so using resources that could help them increase their living standards, but end up instead in weapons which threaten their very existence?

But arms purchases by Third World nations have also directly contributed to their own debts. A report prepared for the Swedish Government in 1987 estimates that 25% of developing countries' debts result from military purchases. The problem tends to increase as more countries come under military rule. In 1960 twenty-two of seventy-eight independent Third World countries were controlled by the military: in 1985 numbers had increased to fifty-seven of 114, with another twenty or thirty where the military were a powerful part of government. The results are usually a higher priority to military as opposed to welfare spending, and frequently, the use of brutal methods in controlling unrest and eliminating opposition. According to Sivard, in 1985, over two thirds of all military governments "resorted to torture, brutality, disappearances and political killings frequently enough to appear to have institutionalised violence as a matter of policy."

The impact of the arms race on the poorest countries of the world has been hardest in the 1980s. The Deputy Secretary General of the Commonwealth said last year,

"The average black African in 1987 has no additional income, will consume no more aid and will have fewer imports than in 1965 – all the gains in income and living standards up to 1980 have been lost in seven years." In the developing world the arms race has created poverty and destitution on a scale that would have been unimaginable twenty years ago. Then, aid was expanding. Now, it is tending to contract. In recent years only four of the industrial nations have reached the United Nations target of 0.7% of GNP – Sweden, Norway, Denmark and the Netherlands. If the United States raised its spending on aid to this target figure it would increase its funding to the poor countries by $25 billion in two years. The World Health Organization estimates that it would cost about $22 billion to provide a safe water supply and sanitation for the world's population.

Is Change Possible?

The arms race of the last forty years has created attitudes so firmly established as to have become almost instincts: of permanent enemies and the acceptance in the industrial world of a misallocation of public funds on a scale that is almost beyond belief. It has allowed the state to gather too much power to itself and led to a decline in democracy. It has slowed and in some cases stopped improvements in living standards. But despite all this there are signs of hope.

1. Between 1950 and 1986 average life expectancy rose from forty-six to sixty-one and the number of literate adults from 66% to 72%.

2. The world's rural population (and most of the world's people are rural) with access to a clean water supply increased from 13% to 44%.

3. Small-pox has effectively been eradicated by a World Health Organization campaign.

Some countries have made great advances.

1. Cape Verde became independent from Portugal in 1975; its economy was in tatters and the physical environment severely degraded, yet in 1987 the World Bank, an organisation not given to praise, said Cape Verde had a 'record of meeting the needs of the poor in the face of adversity that cannot be matched.'

2. Burkina Faso is still one of the very poorest countries, but by concentrating limited resources it was able between 1981 and 1985 to establish a health post in each of its 7,500 villages and reduce infant mortality from 208 to 145 per thousand – unacceptably high, yet a pointer to what can be done if resources are concentrated on basic needs.

3. Laos has increased the literacy rate among women from 36% to 76% over the last five years. Similar results were achieved in Malagasy.

There have also been advances in other areas. Democracy has been revived in Latin America, notably in Argentina and Uruguay. Amnesty International has reported 'significant improvements' in Museveni's Uganda after a very long period of repression under Amin and then Obote.

There are signs of change too in international relations. The agreement between the Soviet Union and the United States on Intermediate Nuclear Forces may not remove many nuclear weapons but – after forty years of failure – it is at least a start to the disarmament process.

Public attitudes have also undergone some changes. As Ferdinand Mount reported in the *Spectator*, the peace movements have influenced public debate on the arms race "by imposing on the policy makers the assumption that the removal of nuclear weapons is the prime moral imperative". Such changes are a small beginning, but they offer hope that the militarised institutions which promote the global arms race can be challenged.

What can be done?

Opportunities abound for individuals and organisations to contribute to changing the international order which keeps the world divided militarily, politically and economically.

1. Campaigns already exist throughout the world promoting the ideas of disarmament and development. Both they and the progressive elements in political parties and trade unions need constantly to look beyond national boundaries and extend international co-operation. This means influencing national foreign policy and increasing its importance with electors.

2. Aggressive arms sales marketing needs to be opposed and international boycotts organised against sales to repressive regimes.

3. Arms conversion projects should be encouraged involving the trade unions and the people working in the defence industries. Part of this conversion could focus on products that would be useful in development.

4. The precedent for nuclear weapons' destruction presented by the INF agreement must be built on and not undermined by "modernisation". The greatest contribution that Britain could make would be to unilaterally remove all nuclear weapons from its territory and to develop non-provocative forms of defence. This action might save the Non-Proliferation Treaty signed in 1968 and now under

great pressure from many near-nuclear states – it would mean at least one of the nuclear powers doing what it promised.

5. Aid to developing countries should quickly be raised to the United Nations target figure and directed to reach the poorest people. Full support should be given to the many international agencies working for change and real development. Aid budgets should only be used on development work and never be diverted for humanitarian famine relief or support for the purchase of arms.

6. There needs to be an acknowledgement by the industrial world of shared responsibility for the debt crisis. The IMF should be reformed to make it into an agent of development rather than simply a cost-cutting organisation.

7. Change must be sought in the attitudes of rich nations. Development cannot succeed if the powerful and wealthy nations continue to back economic dominance with military power in a world of finite resources.

The problems outlined in this book are the most fundamental and urgent facing the world today. Choices are available and have to be made if humankind is to survive. Doctor Bernard Lown MD, the Co-President of the International Physicians for the Prevention of Nuclear War succinctly addressed those choices in his 1983 lecture 'Physicians Confront the Nuclear Peril':

The world today is in danger. But still greater is the opportunity. Although science and technology have catapulted us to the brink of extinction, the same ingenuity has brought humankind to the frontier of the age of abundance. Never before was it possible to feed all the hungry, to shelter all the homeless, to teach all the illiterates, to assuage much of the affliction. Science and medicine can liberate us from drudgery and pain. Only those who can see the invisible can do the impossible. But in order to do the impossible, in the words of Jonathan Schell we ask "not for our personal survival: we ask only that we be survived. We ask for assurance that when we die as individuals, as we know we must, mankind will live on."

We Cannot Plan A Flower: Women and Development

KAMLA BHASIN
NIGHAT SAID KHAN
RITU MENON

Kamla Bhasin has been working with the Food and Agriculture Organization (FAO) of the United Nations for the past thirteen years. Her work focusses on rural development, mainly helping oppressed women and men in South Asia. She deals primarily with non-governmental organizations involved with innovative developmental activities.

Besides the FAO, Kamla Bhasin works closely with several women's organisations.

Nighat Said Khan, a sociologist, is a development consultant and Founder Member of Women's Action Forum, Lahore. She has written a number of papers, pamphlets and research monographs on agrarian reform, development and feminism. She is the Director of Applied Socio-economic Research, Lahore.

Ritu Menon has been in publishing for the last fifteen years, and is Co-Founder of Kali for Women, Indian's first feminist press. Active in the women's movement, she has written on publishing in the Third World and on Women and Media.

I would like to start my presentation with an extract from a prose poem – or not a poem – a reflection – by a friend, Corinne Kumar. This reflection speaks for many of us – as this presentation itself does – for it has been brought together as a synthesis of the questions, the experiences, the struggles, and the reflections of a group of our friends who have been sharing their thoughts on women and development. What I am going to say has been written by three of us. This, then, is *their* presentation as much as it is mine. We hope that by raising these questions in this forum, that we from South Asia; we from the Third World; we women, will start to reach out to each other across the boundaries and the frameworks which now divide us not only from each other, but also within ourselves.

The Awakening Wind

Considering our choices in the Third World
The crisis of our choices
The consequences
Feeling the powerlessness of the impoverished
Understanding that progress, science, development
Mean starvation for millions of people
An escalating armament race
National security ideologies
Nuclear doctrines
That militarize not only our structures

But militarize our minds
A continuum of violence for the women
Thinking of Bhopal
And knowing new deaths and new despair
Realising that thinking is not separate from being
Theory from Practice
Poverty from the poor
Life is not distance from knowledge
The researcher from the researched
The knower not isolated from the known
How can we tell the dancer from the dance?
Going to the women's day demonstration
Thinking of all those limping on the edges of the history
    of man
Crippled for centuries
Dragging the heavy emptiness
Women powerless to name the world
Women without a history
A history without women
Walking with women who have the courage to refuse
Life's humiliations, of degradation
Women bursting forth in collective expressions of
    organising
For water, for wages
Women understanding in the dailiness of our lives
Women protesting dowry, purdah, religious wars
Women struggling for the rights to the land
Women refusing the dogma, the darkness
Sita speaking
Women telling our own stories
Creating the words of our lives
Finding new rhythms
Discovering new roots
Searching for other frames
Other names
A seed here, a flower there
Watching the cosmic canvas and

Anticipating the awakened wind
Perceiving its stirrings
Not knowing the direction
Not determining the texture
Knowing that we cannot plan a flower.

I am sure some of you have heard this parable: there was a factory set up by a rich man – in the name, of course, of national development. The machines in this factory caused many accidents – workers regularly lost their limbs and sometimes their lives.

Some socially conscious people, concerned people, were very moved by the plight of the workers. They felt something needed to be done. They decided a hospital should be set up to provide first aid; the more enlightened ones thought a development project should be set up to rehabilitate the injured workers.

To raise funds they took colour photographs of the mutilated limbs, made posters out of them, and appealed to the emotions of the well-to-do people. People gave – the factory owner himself gave. A very successful project was set up. The factory provided enough wounded people for the hospital and enough work for the social workers.

Those "concerned" with the welfare of the workers only asked questions about how to organise medical aid, and rehabilitation. They did not think it was their business to ask questions like – why is this factory destroying people? Whom does it benefit? In order to keep the factory going for their own benefit they separated politics and development and avoided asking uncomfortable questions.

We believe most of our discussions on women and development have been about the "how" of medical aid rather than the "why" of the accidents in the first place. This we strongly believe needs to be changed.

There is a problem we have with the notion of development – not with the notion itself but with how that notion is interpreted, even by those who do see things holistically. Somehow the word and the concept have become synonymous with economic development. Even among our friends we have had to explain ourselves by using phrases such as "development in its totality" or "holistic development" etc. when we have wanted to talk of development as more than just economic. We wonder why something with so large a canvas that it encompasses the universe, has become so narrow and so rigid.

The word "develop" itself has a wondrous meaning, and is poetic in its implications, for it means to unfold; to unfurl; to unveil, disclose, reveal, discover; to lay open by removal of that which enfolds; to bring out all that is potentially contained therein; to bring forth from latent or elementary conditions; to make manifest what already existed under some other form or condition; to progress; to cause to grow . . .

Likewise development is an unfolding, a bringing in to fuller view that which is latent. It is the production of a natural force, energy, or new form of matter from an existing state to one of a more vigorous, dynamic and creative condition.

In no dictionary will one find the word development explained in economic terms or linked to women in terms of income-generation schemes, food preservation, family planning or skill development – *except*, of course, in the jargon of women and development, which itself is only a derivative of that concept of development that floats around in the corridors of government planning commissions, in UN circles, the World Bank and the International Monetary Fund (IMF), and in bilateral relations. This is the development that addresses itself to Gross National Product; to market forces; to infrastructural development; and to production. In other words, this concept of development is one that is geared to materiality and not to the development of humanity.

116

When we talk of women and development we tend only to talk of women within this narrow definition of growth and to see their development not as an "unfolding of creativity" but in terms of their roles as producers of goods and services (and maybe also as owners some day!).

We reject this narrow definition of development primarily because it is narrow; because it is economistic; and because it not only categorises the human being but also gives greater importance to materiality than to the other more profound aspects of humanity. This concept of development separates the "rational" from the emotional and the spiritual, and makes rationality into a new God.

The focus of this development model, of this one-dimensional concept of progress (be it capitalist or Socialist) has led to the development of the kind of science and technology that has brought the world to the brink of destruction, whether it is the slow destruction of the millions of those starving to death, or the nuclear destruction that will eliminate us all.

We reject this notion of development because the very premise and urges behind it have been wrong and unethical. The main urge seems to have been to control and tame nature, to force it to yield more in the manner man desires – without understanding its own ways of functioning.

Our scientists and development planners have had no values to guide and direct them. This "value-freeness" has been considered a great virtue. "The tragedy of 'modern science' is that it has reduced the categorical imperatives (love, compassion, reverence for life etc.) to relative categories and elevated the relative truth of science to absolute values."

Development and modernisation have meant increasing specialisation, fragmentation, compartmentalisation. I feel the fact that I was invited to talk specifically on women and development perhaps also reflects this frag-

117

mented way of thinking. Why don't we invite an artist, a poet, an actress to talk about development? Aren't their activities part of development? Aren't we also looking at development in very narrow terms?

The kind of development we have is by and for the élite – the masses have not benefited. They have only paid for the development of the better-off sections in their own countries and in the "developed" countries.

It is modern man's insatiable desire to control or at least threaten others which has poisoned our food, wells, paddy fields through the use of fertilisers and pesticides, which has led to the destruction of our forests, which has poisoned our rivers, which has caused Bhopals and Chernobyls and which has posted the demon of nuclear holocaust on our door-steps.

In spite of its obsession with materiality, this concept of development has left several million stomachs empty, half- or semi-filled. In India easily one third of the people live below what is called the poverty line. These millions are for ever hanging between life and death in spite of this growth oriented development. Well, actually – not in spite, but because of this co-called development.

The growth-oriented, capitalist development, directed and controlled by the powerful nations and our own propertied classes, has led to the marginalisation and pauperisation of millions of peasants. It has waged virtual war against the poor by destroying the very resource base on which their survival depends i.e. land, water, forests. It has taken away initiative, self-respect and dignity from the common person. It has reduced people to "targets". From being designers of their own development, they have become its recipients.

This type of development, which has its origins in eighteenth- and nineteenth-century European liberal thinking – not unconnected with European expansionism and colonialism – has created a dominant world view: one where the countries of the North dominate those of

118

the South. Unfortunately, this world view has hegemon-ised the cultures and the civilisations of the Third World.

It has decided our own development; it has given our progress a purely economic face; and it has given us our military states; decided what our scientific signs and symbols must be; and now it is deciding our options for the future.

"Even when this world view talks about alternatives, when it raises the concept of a New International Order, or a North-South dialogue, it still remains within the confines of the economic development model. This model has assumed a universality (even though its origins are Western) and all civilisations of the world are subsumed under it, not only in the economic sphere, but also in terms of all forms of knowledge. All science, for example, is subsumed under one mega science; all medicine under one imperial medicine; all knowledge under something called universal rationality; all economic relation-ships under gross national product; all humanity under materiality.

"This model of development is not only uni-linear and quantitative but it has never been culturally neutral and never gender free. On the contrary it is decidedly Euro-centric, and endro-centric, with patriarchy permeating all aspects of it. The history of this model is a history without women; and the knowledge on which this rationality is based, is a knowledge in which woman is non human. Further-more woman continues to be invisible in this con-struction even when this knowledge is enriched by the social sciences and the humanities." (Corinne Kumar in a talk given at the Second FAO-FFHC/AD South Asian Consultation, March 1987.)

Thus, when we talk about development, even when we talk about it in terms of the development of the people:

119

the development of the poor; and the development of the rural poor, the development of women still forms the underside of it all; the peripheral, the afterthought ... and it is *still* only economic development that we talk about.

Many years ago, C. P. Snow warned us of the creation of two cultures: the culture of science and the culture of humanities, of the increasing chasm between the two, and of the two languages that would result from this separation. Those two cultures are now a reality, and they have created a new version of the haves and have-nots: the men who have and the women who have less and less. And the two languages have brought forth a kind of doublespeak and doublethink that is more danger-ous than any dogma.

When we say peace we mean war, when we say healthy we mean sick, when we say development we mean marginalisation. When our planners talk of progress most of our women experience it as regression. Women's participation in the work force has declined sharply, their access to means of production been systematically denied, their rights to food and shelter become a cruel joke. When our decision-makers talk of better health facilities and increasing life expectancy, our women experience it as forced sterilisation, female foeticide and infanticide and declining sex-ratio. When they talk of self-sufficiency in food our women know that because of the rapacious exploitation of natural resources, there are dangerously diminishing supplies of water, fuel and food and that malnutrition is "as much a matter of what's *under* the pot as of what is *in it*". When our leaders talk of improving the quality of life and working for a better world our women experience it as escalating violence on their persons, the brutalisation of the environment and the sanctioned tyranny of religions and states.

This, then, is our "quarrel" with the concept of women and development because, while it has done much to focus attention on the formerly invisible woman, it still treats women one-dimensionally. Those women involved with this issue are as much to blame for this as the men, for we too have accepted the world view that separates poetry from science; we too have accepted the universal rationality, the one mega science; the one knowledge system. So that when we have attempted to "integrate" women in development we have only worked towards integrating them (and ourselves) into this world view. We have fought many a struggle to "bring women into the main stream"; we have challenged the invisibility of women's contribution to society by conducting countless studies documenting this contribution; we have fought for women's rights to wages and to work; for women's access to the law; and for their rights in decision-making. We have made endless programmes; run countless projects; written numerous reports and books and papers; organised and participated in many conferences, meetings; and all for one end: to acknowledge, to reinforce and to develop the economic contribution of women; to assign a monetary value to it if necessary; and thereby to give women a place in society as if *this* were an end in itself.

But, if we understand that the development of a people is much more than this; if we see that development is, and must be, holistic; if we believe that the essence of development is creativity, then we must move away from this narrow definition of development. We must challenge the very concepts on which these premises are made; we must ourselves be prepared to break free from the frames that we know, the moulds in which we are trapped. We must be prepared to work out our own yardstick, for, as Corinne says in her poem, we have to see that "thinking is not separate from being"; "theory from practice", "the researcher from the researched", "the knower from the known", "the dancer from the dance".

As women, we must start looking for a new vision, an alternative way of developing, and this necessarily means a new construction of knowledge; a new relationship with the poor, with the oppressed, with women. Feminism and the feminist movement is helping us do some of this. It is showing us the possibility of finding new kinds of space, of searching for new ways, finding new frames and new rhythms, of discovering new roots and dreaming new dreams. Feminism is a distinct shift from what has become a universal construct, and it seeks to question and to redefine "progress" and "development", and to work towards a new notion of these in all aspects of our lives.

In many senses this appears to be an unthinkable dream but this dream is only unthinkable for those of us already caught in the one universal world view. For millions of women (and millions of other oppressed people) the feminist vision is no more unthinkable than their dreams of economic security, of justice and humanity, for all of these are as remote from their reality. A majority of the world may be subsumed by the one universal world view, but this majority is not as yet conscious of it, and not as yet actively a part of it. In fact, the feminist vision, and alternative development, may be even closer to their reality than the mega sciences and the nuclear world and may therefore be even more tangible.

For what *is* alternative development, anyway? Very simply, it is a people-based development in that not only the questions, but also the answers come from the people and their own experiences. This means alternative development accepts that there is no one linear development model nor one path to progress. It accepts different logic systems, different idioms, different concepts of time and space. Feminism does all this too. At the same time feminism seeks to break down the barriers between disciplines; between areas of work; between the personal and the political; between the emotional and the logical;

between the natural and the physical; between relationships and roles; between them and us, and between you and me.

If we come close to the people of any Third World country today, if we come close to the oppressed in these countries, we will see that their systems of existence and systems of life are not dissimilar to what alternative development and feminism are attempting to "recreate". The average peasant, the poor, the oppressed, female or male have not yet separated their beings into categories; or their lives into fragments. They have not yet distanced themselves from nature, from spirituality, from emotion, or from what we might call the irrational. They have still not made creativity a different art form. It lingers in all aspects of their lives; the dancer is still not separated from the dance.

This is even more true regarding women. We have often noticed that the women in our countries are much more able to relate to alternatives; much more ready to experiment with new ways of working, and organising and struggling because they have as yet no experiences with the "known" patterns. They have never been a part of a hierarchy or been in positions of power; never been presidents or treasurers or secretaries and therefore are more open to collective decision-making, for instance. In other words, with the majority of women in the Third World countries who are not yet a part of *the* system, we are in the fortunate position of working out "alternative" systems based on their own realities, their own perceptions.

And, in fact, this is exactly what is happening at many, many places now.

In South Asia there are many instances of women's power, their militancy, their unity. Most of these instances are of peasant women, tribal women, urban working-class women who have been in the frontline of struggles against deforestation, mining, usurpation of tribal lands, exploitation by landlords, corruption by bureaucrats, sexual abuse and violence. We now know that in many people's struggles women have been the more daring, the more militant, the more fearless. These women seem to follow the principle "the more you press them down the higher they will rise".

In the North of India, for example, the Chipko hill women participated in a struggle to save trees from being wantonly felled by literally clinging to them, daring the axeman to wield the axe on them first, rather than on the trees. Mass mobilisation was carried out through folk songs which spoke of the life-giving properties of trees and of their role in stabilising the environment, especially the water cycles necessary for hill farming. Over the years, the women have been called upon to resist forest contractors again and again and in the most recent incident some of them physically prevented trucks of felled trees from leaving the forests by throwing themselves in front of them. Contrary to the men, the women have consistently emphasised the ecological rather than the economic aspects of the struggle, a struggle that originally began as a fight against alcoholism. It was this earlier fight that provided them with the organisational base for Chipko.

In Bangladesh we have organisations like NIJERA KORI, which means, we will do it ourselves. NK has helped several thousand rural working-class women to get organised, to fight for their rights, to demand what is theirs and to challenge oppressive structures. Every group decides its own priorities. They have successfully fought to acquire common lands for collective farming, to get higher wages, to get loans, to create better health services, to have rapists punished, to stop pornographic additions in folk theatre. These women have also been using songs and theatre to mobilise and to initiate discussion. Though illiterate, these women are highly intelligent and articulate. In the most graphic of language they talk about the exploitation they are subjected to and the reasons behind it. They speak volumes on patriarchy without even knowing the word. In South Asia there are now very many such organisations of women.

In Nepal we have the Women's Development Programme, initiated by the Government – yet another kind of initiative to start a process of women's development. Through this programme, young educated Nepali women have gone to the most remote villages to live there, to help women form their own groups, and to make plans for their development. The women decide their own priorities. The activists from outside help them realise their plans by facilitating access to information, credit, skills, markets. Once united, these women take on anyone, or anything, which oppresses them.

I could go on telling you about similar success stories of women getting organised to improve their economic conditions, to redefine their social and cultural position, to demand space, dignity, leisure. All kinds of innovative efforts are going on in areas of women's health, education, employment, self-employment, leadership, research. Little lamps of courage and hope everywhere. Attempts are also going on to link these efforts. We have learnt many lessons from these experiments.

We now know that ordinary women and toiling men not only want to but can participate in their own development if they can decide what this development will be. We know that they can be effective leaders and planners of their own development, we know once their creativity is unleashed it cannot be contained. It is this faith in people's power which gives us hope.

We have learnt that development is like a tree: it must grow from below upwards. It cannot be imposed from above. People like you and me can help the people but we cannot and should not try to direct them.

We now know that development means changing the present socio-economic structure; it means redistribution

125

of resources and decision-making power. Every act of ours should challenge the present exploitative structure.

We have learnt that development essentially means empowering the powerless. As power comes through unity, development means the poor getting organised to fight for their rights, to tilt the balance of power in their own favour.

We have learnt that development has to be integrated and multi-dimensional. Therefore development means making links between a lot of like-minded people doing different things. It requires a close partnership between grassroot-level activists, researchers, journalists, artists, planners, lawyers, doctors. Development requires different skills and talents at different levels.

It requires experiments at the micro level and policy changes at the macro level. So a book reinterpreting religion is as important a developmental activity as digging a well.

We have learnt development requires a coming-closer of theory and practices. We have learnt that we need to start talking again of values – like love, equality, honesty, and democracy.

We have learnt that development based on exploitation can only trace a graph of destruction. What, then, is the alternative: we think it is high time that we abandoned our relentless pursuit of surplus and looked instead for sustainability; that we stopped being preoccupied with quantitative changes and started genuinely looking for and making qualitative ones; that we shifted the focus from what an Indian woman ecologist calls male development – mal-development – to a woman-centred development. We think this shift is critical.

We should stop trying to integrate women in to mal-development and make a fundamental shift in our perspective of locating women centrally in this process of reconstruction, of understanding that a development programme without women at its centre is no programme at all.

Let me return to the example of the Chipko women. The lesson they have taught us is the lesson of conservation; of the interdependence of nature and human beings, of a holistic rather than a fragmented development, of the value of food crops over cash crops, of the necessity to sustain life-support systems, not plunder them. I would like to suggest that women, as much as soil, water and forests, are a life-support system.

So, friends, I conclude with the plea: let us think of women and development differently, holistically, creatively. Let us try to regain the real meaning of development, i.e. to bring into fuller view that which is latent. Let us think of growth as organic growth and let our efforts only be to unleash the creativity of women so that they themselves can design their own development. Let us see our efforts only in terms of sowing a seed, and let us not forget that we cannot plan a flower.

The Importance of Women in Development

SITHEMBISO NYONI

Sithembiso Nyoni is a rural development activist in Zimbabwe. A Co-Ordinator of a Village Development Movement within the Organisation of Rural Associations for Progress (ORAP), she is currently training village youths in record-keeping and the documentation of village experiences. Drawing on her own experience of grassroot groups, Sithembison Nyoni has already written several published articles on participation, women and other development issues.

Sithembiso Nyoni is the first woman to sit on two of Zimbabwe's national boards – the Derelict Lands Board in the Ministry of Agriculture, and the Board of the Forestry Commission under the Ministry of Natural Resources and Tourism.

The situation and plight of women the world over has been on the world agenda for almost one and a half decades. Some research and numerous seminars have been held and there is vast documentation on women. This includes the role played by women in the reproduction, nurturing and sustenance of society. It has been proven beyond doubt that most nations would have collapsed without the contribution of their women. The examples I know best are those of the African continent. The economies and social fabrics of most African nations especially in some West and East African countries would have collapsed without their market women. Those of southern Africa, such as Zimbabwe, would not have won the liberation war without women and would have had serious food shortages without the women agricultural producers. The list of women's contributions to society is long and well known. For this reason I shall not dwell on it.

This chapter tries to question the importance of women in development. It tries to examine whether or not women themselves, as well as all those who support their cause, really understand what their importance means. For decades women's contributions have been said to be both necessary and important. If this is so, then I wonder why the plight of the majority of women has not changed. The role of women in development as it stands today may be necessary but is it really important?

Let us first examine the word important. The *Oxford Advanced Learners' Dictionary of Current English* defines important as: "of great influence; to be treated seriously; having great effect and having a position of authority". Are the contributions of women as mothers, home-makers, agricultural producers, project-holders etc. of great influence to society? Are all the roles and positions allotted to women treated seriously? Do they have great effect on society, and have positions of authority? If the answer to these questions is no, as it clearly is, then it stands to reason that women's contributions to development are only necessary, not important.

The challenge for me therefore, is not for us as women to surface and present well what women do or contribute, then try to persuade or force society to accept that as important, but rather to question whether we are indeed One World in which both men and women must participate and live as equal citizens. If this concept of One World is accepted, then we need to sort out all the factors which make our One World tick, and separate those which are necessary from those which are important, then make sure that there is an equal gender distribution of labour, income, development benefits and positions etc.

Women have been marginalised and oppressed for too long. For too long they were made to believe that their contribution to society was "important" until they themselves were unable to distinguish between necessity and importance. Necessity does not necessarily empower an individual, but importance often leads to influence, being taken seriously and to positions of authority, and it thus empowers people either to be themselves or to change their world.

Women have also been made to believe that they are naturally more sensitive, kinder and have more highly developed emotions than men. Because they have been made to believe that it is their natural and God-given role to love and care, they tend to accept positions of performing necessary tasks without question. They have been conditioned not to let humanity down. They then find themselves trapped into doing all the household and the societal chores which are often neither paid nor important in the local and national decision-making machinery.

This situation is often perpetuated by the education and training women get. Women's education and training prepares them to perform their God-given positions well both at home and in society. Their training has thus concentrated on practical skills such as typing, office management, sewing, home improvements, vegetable gardening etc. In rural development, for instance, women are taught to expect concrete results from their training. Their organisations often offer reliable practical programmes usually lacking in continuity. By accepting this kind of training women often encourage the perpetuation of training schemes which prevent them from performing and entering into important development tasks and positions.

Closely related to education is woman's economic position and the question of whether or not she has access to the means of production. As long as women producers, for example, have no access to land, water, credits and markets, their food production will remain "necessary" rather than "important".

I would like to cite one example: Zimbabwe, the country I know best. Before independence in 1965, women had no rights to land or credits. After independence the laws changed to include women. As a result, the maize production of communal farmers, the majority of whom are women, rose from 6% in 1979 to 50% in 1986–87. Access to land and credit changed the status of most women from disregarded subsistence farmers to important producers. Such women are not only taken seriously but have also acquired some production and economic power. They can, then, be said to be playing an important role in the development of their country.

As long as women are not part of the important development issues and processes surrounding agriculture, trade, industry, energy, finance, science and technology, they will never play an important role in development and will always be on the periphery of society's decision-making processes as regards development benefits. They need also to engage in the politics of development. Women can no longer afford to accept their role as stereotypes, nor can they continue to be pushed into positions of slavery and powerlessness.

In every society it is the women who are at the bottom of the economic, social and political piles. In these positions they are left with no means to make a living. Women find themselves devising all sorts of strategies for survival. These include some methods of child care, food production and preservation, organising specific issues for self-help and giving each other and those around them some psychological, spiritual and physical support such as is happening in Soweto in South Africa.

In their struggle for survival women have accumulated a lot of development knowledge upon which some development strategies have been based. Only when such knowledge has received national recognition and has been channelled into an institution have women been taken seriously and thus been seen as important to development. The three examples given below show that in recent years a lot of women's and other development organisations have sprung up in many countries in response either to the plight of the poor sectors of society or purely to women.

The Organisation of Rural Associations for Progress (ORAP) in Zimbabwe was founded by a woman soon after independence and has since grown into a big grassroot movement. Its brief is to mobilise the rural sector into development action through new awareness and institution-building for themselves. Development dialogue and education are central to ORAP's work. Some breakthrough has also been made in the area of food production and distribution as mentioned previously. It has created a rural membership which understands that its development, and indeed that of its nation, cannot come about through projects alone but more importantly, when it takes its rightful place and position as citizens of Zimbabwe, participating fully in all areas of national development and decision-making processes.

In 1982 rural people, especially women, identified one of the causes of hunger and food shortage as maldistribution of food. They then approached the Ministry of Agriculture asking to be given a permit to buy food direct from each other as small village producers instead of through the Grain Marketing Board. Their request was granted. After four years' experience of buying and selling food direct, rural communities so refined their system that in the 1986–87 drought the Government asked them to take up the responsibility of distributing food to a whole province of Matabeleland South. Over 1,200 tons of maize are now being distributed to various rural points per month, ensuring that as many families as possible have access to food.

The Government Public Works Programme, "Food-for-Work", is now dependent on the ORAP food programme to provide food for purchase in some villages. The Government had provided jobs for people to earn cash to buy food. However, because of the maldistribution of food in some remote rural areas there would often be nothing to buy. By improving distribution, people in rural areas created an interdependence with the Government, where their contribution became important to the state.

There are other examples of women's development organisations springing up: in Bolivia, the Aymara Women's Organisation of Kollasuyo was formed by women in response to discrimination against them and their consequently lowly positions in society.

It is a very new organisation which has been said to

have great potential for making a very important contribution to the development of the Aymara people as well as that of the Bolivian society.

"Rural Women in Latin America" put their case as follows: "In the towns Aymara women suffer discrimination at every level; as Aymara, as women and as economical outcasts.

"Over the years education, the church and the media have combined to erode our traditional way of life and undermine women's role with it . . .

"We have realised the need to locate a specifically female organisation in order to work to restore our Aymara way of life.

"We are motivated by the sad predicament of Aymara women and the misery to which our communities have been reduced, our hungry children and our collective demoralization. We work because we have seen the suffering of our people." (Pp. 64-6 *Rural Women in Latin America*, Isis International 1987.)

The Women's Action Centre was born out of the extensive work of two women in the poor sectors of Guayaquil, Ecuador's chief seaport and most populated city. From the beginning the main purpose of the centre was to focus on the problems of women in the poor districts of Guayaquil. As their problems, especially those of peasant women who had migrated from the city, became more dramatic, it became imperative for such a project to be formed with the intention of responding to their needs. It is run by women for women.

In 1982 CAM obtained legal standing from the Ministry of Social Welfare. Those who have become involved in this organisation have been able to build the foundations for freedom, although their struggle is far from being over.

The above examples form only a fraction of what women all over the world have been able to do through their hard-earned organisational skills. It is very common, however, that as soon as women's initiatives move from being survival strategies into powerful economic, political or cultural entities, men take them over and control them to the detriment of women. This is true of most income-generating activities in the developing world. Cooking, washing up, laundry, food processing etc. are women's work. But as soon as they become economically viable or commercialised, men take them over and eventually gain economic and political control in society through them. In most African countries, women and the young are in the centre of political mobilisation and they are the major voters, yet their names are never put forward as candidates, nor are they given any important positions as civil servants. In the world of non-governmental organisations most development agencies are headed by men – in some cases, even those which were initiated by women.

Thus, even in development circles, women do most of the work and yet are still pushed into rendering necessary services rather than playing an important part in the shaping and implementation of their national development goals.

Because women all over the world share similar experiences, though varying in degree, they cannot afford to be segmented. Unity is strength. The systems and mechanisms which are used to undermine women may be different in each country or cultural setting but they all lead women to similar situations of poverty, deprivation and powerlessness.

Some women have allowed themselves to be used against other women in political and economic areas. Others have climbed to higher positions through the male game of oppression and manipulation. It is my belief that women have vast experience and knowledge which, if harnessed and put together, could be used to create new national and international value systems as well as new relationships upon which development for all can be based. This, however, demands that women form a new image of themselves, not as second-class citizens only capable of performing the necessary chores but as full human beings called to be part of One World and to participate in all their national development tasks.

As seen above, integration and importance in development cannot be *given* to women. They have to *struggle* for it. Women need to identify their abilities and capabilities and develop them to the full. They need to turn their survival strategies and household chores into national and international development strategies as shown above.

Women need to fight to be able to make an important contribution to development, to occupy positions of influence which enable them to play an effective role in society and to have the means by which to change their situation. With the sensitive and caring qualities of women recognised as integral to such positions, women could change the world for the better.

These good qualities which are, however, used to subjugate women and reduce them to occupying only survival roles are needed at all levels of society. They can no longer be confined only to the subsistence levels of women's operations. They should be exercised by all concerned. Some political and economic powers have lost basic human values of democracy, caring, sharing and equality. These powers would rather put economic and political gains before justice and human rights. There is evidence all around us of a world which is falling apart because of national and international decisions based on political and economic interests rather than on human dignity based on equality and improved quality of life.

The importance of women in development is a must. The world cannot continue to marginalise women and neglect their invaluable contribution to changing and to stabilising nations. Women themselves need to work out what is important to society as opposed to what is necessary. They need to develop new educational and training strategies for themselves so as to increase their critical analysis of their societies, and thus increase their social awareness. They should refuse society-defining roles and development positions created specifically for them. Women need to understand the total situation around them and then define and occupy positions not only as individuals but also as a collective, looking to what is important to the development of their nations.

It is true that women hold half the sky. What needs to be examined, however, is this; as what are women holding the sky? And how are they doing it? Women have generated a lot of the world's wealth and have accumulated valuable knowledge skills and experiences. But how are these being used? By whom? To what end?

It is true that behind every powerful and successful man or nation is a powerful woman. But for how long will women allow themselves to be used as stepping stones and supporting pillars of national policies which continue to empower only one section of society to their detriment? For how long are they prepared to go on as shadows of power and development?

It is true that aid given to women is development aid for generations to come. But what is the nature of this assistance? How is it given and for what? Rural women and those in poor sectors of society want to be taken seriously. They want to be part of their societies not targets of development aid.

The issue is not only to provide a well for village women to walk fewer miles to their water points, facilitate a sewing group for squatter families or meals on wheels for the homeless, but rather to question why such women have no water, no income and no homes. Such assistance is needed to alleviate pain and suffering but cannot provide permanent solutions for the plight of such women.

The challenge to society is that such families need to

regain their rights to water, jobs and shelter, and not to remain as development targets but as important participants. Development assistance which merely aids and abets women's survival chores can only be short term. If it is given as an end in itself it serves as an oppressive tool to keep women on the margins of society performing all the "necessary" chores.

Such assistance should be given as a step towards moving women into performing integrated, socially valued and thus important development tasks.

Women need to develop new games and strategies which their mothers never taught them and turn their valuable contributions into important development ventures. The potential importance of women in development cannot be over-emphasised.

Organising Self-Employed Women for Self-Reliance in India

ELA BHATT

Ela Bhatt is a social worker and women's activist who has written extensively on the need to prioritise women's roles in development programmes throughout India. She is the General Secretary of the Self-Employed Women's Association (SEWA) in Ahmedabad, India, and an active Member of Parliament.

Ela Bhatt has received the Magsaysay Award for Community Leadership, the Susan Anthony Award for National Integration, and the Right Livelihood Award, also known as the Alternative Nobel Prize.

Here is a story of people making headway in the streams of national development while constantly defending their rightful place in the economy and the society. They are the self-employed women of India. I have been involved with their movement from the beginning, and I would like to give you an account of their work and struggles to achieve self-reliance, economically and mentally.

SEWA (Self-Employed Women's Association; also "service" in many Indian languages) is an organisation in Ahmedabad, in the state of Gujarat, of 22,745 self-employed women workers (1985 figures). Having grown out of the Women's Wing of the Textile Labour Union in Ahmedabad, it is a registered trade union in its own right. Gandhian thinking is the guiding force for us. We visualise a society in which capital and labour are dispersed, and none is deprived of the capital needed to survive. We operate primarily through the joint action of labour unions and co-operatives, and our goals are to organise and create visibility for self-employed women, enabling them to receive higher wages and to have control over their own income. SEWA has spread into six other states as well, and has reached a total of about 40,000 women workers (as at 1985).

After this brief background, let me begin with some profiles of the self-employed women and the reality of their situation.

1. A vegetable vendor borrows Rs 60 ($5) from a private money lender early in the morning, buys vegetables,

trades them in the whole day and afterwards returns Rs 70 ($6) to the money lender. This goes on day after day. Three generations ago her family had their own land in the village, grew vegetables there, and would make daily trips to the city to sell their produce. The ruler at that time had given a very large market space to the vegetable vendors. But with the coming of textile mills and other industrial units, it was gradually taken over by residential houses and retail shops. Today she and the other vendors are literally pushed into the street.

2. A patchworker gets rags of textile-mill waste from a private trader to stitch into quilt covers, using her own sewing machine, thread, and labour. She is paid RS10 ($1) per quilt cover, and is able to stitch six of them a day.

3. A junksmith buys metal scrap and waste from a scrap dealer to make crude pots, containers, and other household utility items. Working with primitive tools, she must hammer twenty to thirty times just to cut a hole in a metal sheet.

4. A farm labourer toils eight to ten hours a day and earns Rs10 ($1). Agricultural work provides income only for a few months in the year, thus making her vulnerable to indebtedness and consequent passive acceptance of low wages to repay loans. Up until the last decade, her family wove cloth for their own consumption and also for sale during the slack season. However, the growth of the textile industry in Ahmedabad and other parts of Gujarat took away much of the handloom weavers' market and yarn for weaving became scarcer. Most of the weavers have become farm labourers; some migrate to the city and make a living picking wastepaper from the streets.

The list of trades is long, the examples of self-employed are numerous. But these illustrations describe the plight of a vast number of economically active women who are the invisible workers of the nation, and also of the world. They rarely own capital or tools of production, they have no direct link with organised industry and services, and they have no access to modern technology or facilities. All they possess is the skills and knowledge of their trade and their physical labour. They constitute the majority of the enormous population of self-employed workers, normally called the 'unorganised sector'. In India only 6% of working women are in organised industry and services; the remaining 94% are left to fend for themselves.

Self-employment

A major form of work and of earning a livelihood in our country, self-employment is usually meant to include individuals who work independently to produce goods or services which are sold for a price. (Employment, on the other hand, generally defines people who work in regular salaried jobs for somebody else in an employer-employee relationship.)

Historically, the people in our country have been essentially self-employed. In traditional societies most work is done on a subsistence level, each family having to provide its basic needs – food, clothing, shelter – from its own resources, usually by hand. Very few people work for others in an employer-employee relationship, although trading, artisanry and priestly services, for instance, are performed for the community in a patron-client relationship. Among nomadic and tribal communities particularly, a strong relationship develops with nature and land, be it forest, oasis, or sea, or a pattern of *jhum* (slash-and-burn) cultivation. This was the case in India until the last century – and even today we find patches of such societies in some parts of the country.

With the Industrial Revolution, the modes of production shift from work being done by hand to work being done by machines, from work being done in individual homes to work being done in factories. More people, then, are forced to work for others. Concentration of resources increases rapidly in the hands of a few owners, and exploitation becomes rampant. The modern labour movement starts as a response to this rampant exploitation, and the state is influenced to protect those in employment, formulating and enforcing laws, rules, and regulations for them. The employer–employee relationship becomes more and more established, and organised industry, organised labour and organised services become more and more significant in the economy. In India the trade unions, the laws pertaining to employer–employee relationships, the role of the state in safeguarding the interests of the employees have all been based on the models of the highly industrialised countries. In these countries the process of industrialisation has continued for over two hundred years and slowly brought most of the working population into regular salaried employment. The rules relating to employment thus ensure the interests of almost the whole working population.

India's traditional economy – only partially commercialised, largely agricultural and tribal, and subsistence-based – has now had superimposed on it an industrial economy. The concentration of resources has made a large majority of the subsistence-oriented population resourceless, and the new technologies that are constantly coming into existence displace more and more of them. At the same time, since the economy as a whole has not become industrialised, not everybody finds regular salaried employment – the labour movement having catered mainly to industrial labour. Today in our country only 11% of the working people are engaged in regular jobs with a recognised employer–employee relationship, the protection of the law, and the benefits that this brings. Eighty-nine percent must earn their livelihood by creating their own niche in the economy. If the strength of regular employment is security of work and money, this very substantial population has neither.

A subsistence economy gives equal recognition to the work of men and women. With commercialisation, the work that can generate cash income becomes more highly valued. In addition, the new skills introduced by industrialisation and mechanisation have gone primarily to men, forcing the work of women into less and less skilled areas and making it seem less and less important. So women in particular have suffered from the changing economic structure, because they are self-employed workers and because they are women.

Culture of Self-Employment

Every form of work develops its own culture. In our traditional society, a strong underlying culture that is associated with self-employment has evolved through the ages. Small communities of people engaged in subsistence-oriented work were common. Direct communication with distant places was not possible. As a result transactions, decisions, payments and negotiations were accomplished with relatively few known people, face to face, fostering a sense of trust and allowing agreements to be verbal. In such a world there is no real need for the written word. You can live your life comfortably without feeling inadequate or helpless, dependent or exploited because you do not read and write, and our people for this reason have not felt handicapped by illiteracy. This is not to say that the written word was unknown in our traditional system – the scriptures were written, treasury accounts were written, the firmans of kings were written – but writing was only for a few.

Another important characteristic of the culture of self-employment is its sense of time. Fixed schedules, dates, and deadlines do not figure prominently in our traditional work system (they do, however, in our social life) except for the computation of suitable hours for performing certain activities, occasions to mark the seasons, and festivals.

This culture of small communities has been affected by the processes of centralisation – of larger and larger geographical areas coming under common administration (e.g., the formation of kingdoms and nations) and the establishment of large-scale commercial enterprises during the last fifty to seventy years – of industrialisation, of growing employment as described above. What characterises the newer culture of employment is a different discipline with respect to time that is difficult for many to cope with, and written, impersonal dealings with unknown people that follow from the economic units of larger scale.

Although some of the work force have become integrated into this culture, the self-employed – who are mostly poor – are being forced to deal with the unfamiliar world of written transactions. Their illiteracy and their ignorance of written laws, etc., has become a major handicap for them. They do not know how to get things done in this system, and they end up being exploited. Do we realise the crucial reality of our people? Our SEWA women feel annoyed and sometimes afraid when they receive printed letters at home. "Don't you trust us, that you write letters to us?" they ask. All our programmes and schemes for poverty alleviation, for development, for improving the lives of the people are planned assuming that everyone is familiar with the workings of written records, applications, evidence and authentications. But this assumption is false. Naturally, only those who know about and have access to them receive the benefits of the programmes, while the people for whom they are really intended are at the mercy of the kingpins who are at home in both worlds, written and verbal.

How will we progress as a people, how will we tackle exploitation and the distance between the rich and the poor unless we recognise the characteristics of our culture? Why do we impose formal structures on it and use them as the measure of our progress? We have to devise ways of making the verbal world valid even in officialdom, ways of keeping illiteracy from preventing our people to improve their lives and situations. We have to develop forums for the illiterate and literate to hold hands without exploitation.

Self-Employed Workers

These people have been referred to by various names: "unorganised", "informal", "marginal", "unregulated", "peripheral", "residual". Such negative terms give them an inferior and insignificant position in the economy, whereas in fact they are in the centre of it and contribute a great deal. To give them positive status and to draw positive attention towards them, we call them self-employed workers.

Broadly speaking there are three categories of self-employed workers:

1. Small-scale vendors, petty traders and hawkers selling goods such as vegetables, fruits, fish, eggs and other staples, household goods, garments and similar types of products.

2. Home-based producers making such articles as *bidi*s (tobacco leaves rolled into cigarette form), *agarbatti*s (incense sticks), garments, small furniture, footwear, fabric and handicrafts.

3. Labourers selling various kinds of services, including cleaning, laundering, catering, cooking, helping

to care for the sick or providing labour for construction, transportation, agriculture or other activities.

The limited amount of data available makes it difficult
to assess the size or composition of the self-employed
sector. However, over the past few years SEWA has
conducted a series of socio-economic surveys of self-
employed women. We have learned that for a great
majority (78%), capital for initial financing and day-to-
day operating costs is their own or comes from relatives,
merchants, or private money lenders, not banks. Their
daily earnings are minimal and hence many (60%) remain
in debt. Most (78%) rent their means of labour such as
*larri*s (hand carts).

Despite long hours of work, productivity is low due to
a broad range of social, economic, and even legal constraints. Many self-employed women are illiterate, and
most (97%) live in temporary settlements in city slums.
Twenty-one to 33% of the women are household heads,
and children accompany 70% of them to the worksite.
They have extremely limited access to raw materials,
markets, training and space for the production and/or
sale of goods besides. In sum, the self-employed must
work long hours under difficult circumstances to eke out
a bare minimum living.

The self-employed sector comprises a substantial proportion of the urban work force (45% in Calcutta, 40% in
Bombay, 55% in Ahmedabad). Millions of people, then,
mainly in the low-income groups (women, children,
scheduled castes and tribes and backward classes), are
self-employed. Further, many of the goods and services
consumed by the general population are provided by this
sector. As such, there is ample justification for focussing
on this group in programmes aimed at expanding employment opportunities, increasing income, and raising productivity. Any labour movement worth its name must
include them and help them share in the fruits of prosper-

ity. And if we want to have a women's movement in India, all of the economically active women, whether they are rural or poor or work at home, should play a role.

We tried to organise self-employed women workers into a trade union, viz. The Self-Employed Women's Association, in 1972.

Struggles for Self-Reliance and a Trade Union

The first struggle waged by SEWA was for its own registration under the Trade Union Act. "You cannot be a trade union," said the Registrar, "because you are not workers: you do not have an employer. Against whom are you going to agitate?" We argued, "A worker is not only an employee. A worker is a person who earns his/her living by his/her own effort without exploiting the labour of others." We pointed out as well that "a trade union is not always against an employer, but for the solidarity of the workers, for their own development. A worker is oppressed not only by an employer but by many other sections of society and vested interests." Ultimately the Registrar accepted our defence and did register SEWA as a trade union. Today SEWA is affiliated with two Internationals, the International Union of Food and Tobacco Workers (IUF), Geneva, and the International Farm Plantation Allied Workers (IFPAW), Geneva.

Vendors and Hawkers

Manekchowk is the main vegetable market of Ahmedabad city. Vendors and hawkers have been selling in Manekchowk Square for the last three generations, each family in its traditional space. As the city has grown, the square has become more and more crowded, and pedestrians, cars, cycles, rickshaws, handcarts and vendors jostle each other in the limited area. In January 1980 the city authorities decided to reduce the congestion by removing all of the vendors from the market. Hundreds of women were thus displaced from employment. They approached the authorities, but talks proved futile, as the authorities were determined to throw the vendors out. So the vendor sisters organised a *satyagraha*, occupying their places in peaceful defiance of the police orders. In spite of the strong opposition from the police, municipality, and large shopkeepers and traders, the vendors sat firmly united. Their defensive action won back their old place in Manekchowk.

But this was not a permanent solution. Three vendor leaders and SEWA had to file a writ petition to the Supreme Court in February 1982 seeking social justice for the vendors of Manekchowk. SEWA's plea was that we are an integral part of the market, having been there far longer than the shops, houses, buildings, roads, and so we should be given licence to sell there. Another demand was to make the market square a pedestrian zone, free of all vehicular traffic. The Supreme Court issued a stay order at the first hearing in 1982 and asked the Municipal Corporation to prepare a suitable scheme to seat the vendors in the market. A proposed model was discussed, and mutually agreed. The 1984 judgment giving licences and assuring space to each of the vendors in the existing market has proved a turning point in present urban policy with respect to the status of hawkers in big cities.

"We are giving a useful service to city dwellers," say the vendor sisters. "We are respectable traders, though small. We will not be treated as criminals." However, the negative attitudes towards them are very deeply entrenched. The middle-class citizens look down upon the vendors as dirty, loud, and uncultured. The authorities and planners see them as nuisances and traffic obstructions rather than as a necessary part of the city. But at least the Supreme Court order has changed the behaviour of the town planners. A new, modern market is being built in consultation with SEWA, in Manek-chowk, for the vendors.

Defending Motherhood

Kankuben, twenty-five years old, is an agricultural labourer in a village in Ahmedabad district. She is in the ninth month of pregnancy but must continue to go to work to earn the daily meal for her family. When she feels her labour pains, she comes home and her sister-in-law calls the midwife. Kankuben has neither the time to go to the hospital – because she knows she must be back at work within a week – nor the money. The baby is born in unhygienic conditions and dies of tetanus. Kankuben is ill for many days and unable to work. There is little or sometimes no food in the house, and her children are hungry. When she does return to work she is weak and cannot earn much. Why should Kankuben and others like her be penalised for motherhood? How can they defend their right to have a child under proper medical care without foregoing their daily earnings?

SEWA feels that we as women are providing for the continuity of society, so motherhood should not be seen as a burden to be borne by women alone. With this conviction we went to the insurance companies and asked, "During the time of delivery a mother has to stop working and earning. Can you create a scheme which will protect her motherhood?" The insurance companies tried, but in the end replied, "No, women are a high insurance risk and poor women particularly so, since so many of them die. We cannot afford to insure them unless we charge a very high premium." No other agency could help us. SEWA then started its own motherhood defence, the Maternity Benefit Scheme.

Mothers are provided cash for immediate expenditures,

lost work pay, medicines and nourishment to replenish them after giving birth. The death rate among mothers under the scheme has fallen. The Government of Gujarat subsequently adopted the scheme on a pilot scale for agricultural workers. We hope that motherhood defence will reach the working mothers all over the country.

Financial Services

Self-employed women face two most common economic problems: their means of production are hired, and they are short of capital. They are therefore always vulnerable to exploitation. During the early 1970s our banks were nationalised, and that held out hope for the poor to obtain loans and credit.

But providing finances to the women was not simple. We were inexperienced and so were the banks, at that time lacking the conceptual clarity, technical know-how, and trained personnel to serve the poor. Along with our recommendations, there was continuous pressure from central government for local banks to give loans to "small" borrowers, and so one of the major banks in Ahmedabad took the first step and made loans to about five hundred SEWA women; then many more banks followed suit.

Nevertheless, the members still faced a number of practical difficulties. There was the problem of bridging the gap between women in filthy clothes, accompanied by noisy children, and the bank staff, in their neckties and air-conditioned offices, who were used to educated, middle-class clients. Then the women's heavy schedule did not permit them to keep to banking hours. If the bank refused to accept payment at the time of day when the women were free to come, the money was spent – or too often deposited with the very wholesaler or money lender from whose clutches SEWA was trying to rescue the women, because they wanted to protect the loan money from the greedy eyes of their husbands or sons. In short, they had no secure place for their spare cash.

It became quite obvious to us that providing money from the bank was just a beginning. If the self-employed are really to be served, they should not only have credit facilities but also an institutional framework offering various other kinds of services that they sorely lack. The question before us was how to achieve this. At a meeting in December 1973, the members enthusiastically came forward with an answer, "a bank of our own", where they would be accepted in their own right and not made to feel inferior. "We are poor, but we are so many!" they said. With determination, 4,000 women contributed share capital of Rs. 10 each to establish the Shri Mahila SEWA Sahakari Bank (Women's Co-operative SEWA Bank). The SEWA Bank was born against stiff opposition and resistance from the banking system. They thought that a bank for poor, illiterate, self-employed women – who in their view were undependable and not responsible for any financial decisions in their family – was a disastrous and suicidal attempt. "How can women, who cannot even sign their names, have a bank account?" they objected. We dealt with this by using photographs instead of signatures for identification – that is, a photograph of the borrower was pasted on her passbook and a copy of that photo was kept in the bank records instead of the specimen signature card. Through this device we avoided forgery or cheating, and in the most Gandhian way we could also non-violently eliminate husbands from managing their wives' accounts. Then, when the members found out that eleven promoters had to sign the registration papers, the illiterate group leaders sat up through a night to learn to write their names without error! In May 1974, the SEWA Bank was registered as a co-operative bank.

Since then we have shattered the existing myths about

155

banking with poor, illiterate women and proved it to be a viable financial venture. At the end of 1984, SEWA Bank had 20,122 savings accounts (99% of holders were illiterate) with about Rs. 1 crore ($800,000) as working capital. The loan repayment rate is more than 98%. SEWA Bank and credit fund make available the other supportive services inevitably needed to make the loan productive: training in management of money, counselling in purchase and marketing of goods, legal aid, maternal protection and life insurance. And most importantly, through its savings accounts, the Bank provides the women with a secure and exploitation-free way to control their own income.

A Complex of SEWA Co-operatives

The idea for organising co-operatives originally grew out of our union's involvement in the struggles of women *chindi* (textile rag) workers, hand-block-printers, and bamboo workers. After years of being victimised by merchants, over six hundred patch workers gathered together in 1977 to exert pressure for payment of minimum wages. By all rights, this was not an unreasonable demand, and after a long series of negotiations a compromise was reached between the two groups. However, within twenty-four hours the merchants broke the agreement. Not only did they refuse to pay the women the agreed-upon rate for sewing the *chindi*, they began to harass the workers by giving them bad materials to sew, less work, and in many cases withholding work from them altogether, especially those who were the sole supporters of their family.

So with SEWA's backing, these women decided to start a production unit of their own. SEWA's work in organising hand-block-printers brought to light the serious dislocation they were facing due to a declining market for

156

their traditional textile designs. In organising bamboo workers, SEWA found that although they were highly skilled, the women were not making products and designs for which the modern market was expanding, but instead were turning out crude products which were sold to merchants at low prices. The women had no means by which to upgrade their skills so that they could produce goods in high demand in the market for higher returns. Through our experience with these and other trade groups the need became evident for alternative institutions through which poor, self-employed women could acquire skills, training, and assistance in marketing finished products, purchasing raw materials, securing storage and work space and acquiring capital.

Sabina *Chindi* Co-operative

For years, Muslim textile rag workers had been sewing for traders on dilapidated machines to make *khol*s (quilts) that fetched the trader low prices and brought the women low wages. SEWA conducted a survey of these women in the Dariyapur neighbourhood in Ahmedabad, and subsequently organised them to demand fair wages, with the consequences described previously. They formed their own production unit, with just one 50-kilogram bag of *chindi*, in 1978. What began with a survey led to liberation of these Muslim women from vested interests.

Today the Sabina Co-operative has a shop in Dariyapur, right alongside the very merchants against whom it had fought. The shop is mostly managed by *khol*-makers themselves.

Because the financial crisis in the textile industry has closed down mills, the co-operative has been facing difficulties in obtaining raw material, and thus in earning income. To overcome this problem women are being trained in making fancy patchwork and appliqué items out of textile rags for the urban market. They continue to produce rag *khol*s for rural and urban poor when the raw material is available.

The Block-Printers' Co-operative "Aabodana"

'Aabodana' consists of Chhipa Muslim women. Prior to the formation of the co-operative the women were block-printing fabrics for wholesale traders. They worked at home, with the cloth, blocks, and dyes provided by the traders. The women were unaware of how the fabrics they produced were marketed or what price they fetched; they were just labourers paid at meagre piece rates – i.e., Rs. 1 ($.08) for three bed covers – and they helplessly accepted this situation as their skills were so limited.

Along with the diminishing consumption of block-printed clothes by tribal men, for example, who switched from printed loincloths to trousers, and middle-class Bania women, who took to wearing plain white saris during mourning periods instead of block-printed saris, the advent of screen printing led to a real crisis for the block-printers. The screen-printed fabrics have a far lower sale price because they can be mass produced. The block-printers – all of them women – were thus rendered unemployed.

One of the block-printers learned that SEWA Bank was offering loans to buy sewing machines. In an effort to find alternative employment some Chhipa women came to SEWA for help. This prompted SEWA to take a survey of the block-printers, and it revealed their appalling socio-economic conditions. With the assistance of the All India Handicrafts Board a training programme was organised to broaden their skills. Despite resistance not only from the traders and the families of the women but initially from the craftsmen, too, who were reluctant to impart the techniques of printing to women, they succeeded through the programme in acquiring proficiency in the entire process of producing block-printed material, from mixing of dyes (including the use of vegetable dyes, a long-lost traditional craft) to post-printing processes.

Since the Chhipa women did not want to work again for the middlemen or to sit at home unemployed, the next logical step for them was to form a production unit where they could work for ensured regular income. The stage was set to convert this production unit into a co-operative.

'Aabodana', registered in 1983, is run by a worker-manager aided by a team of co-operative members. They are working hard to get orders and sell directly to consumers also, and are hopeful of becoming financially self-sufficient.

Cane and Bamboo Co-operative "Baansri"

A chance meeting with a woman from the Bansfodia community (cane and bamboo workers) during a bus journey made by one of our SEWA organisers revealed the grim plight of this community. They were buying raw materials at high prices and getting minimal returns from the sale of their products, i.e., Rs. 3 ($.25) per day. Home-based workers, they make primitive cane and bamboo articles like baskets and brooms. The bamboo they used was long, their homes tiny, and so they had to sit on the roadside to work, causing some traffic obstruction and leading to police harassment. Apart from space their problem was lack of access to raw material, since it was used for industrial purposes.

SEWA organised them to work in a group and created a training programme for them in collaboration with the All India Handicrafts Board. They learned to make a variety of articles for the modern market, from pin cushions and bangles to pieces of furniture. They have now formed themselves into a co-operative, registered in 1983, and they supply brooms and baskets to all government institutions and offices.

Paper Pickers' Co-operative "Sujata"

For hundreds of Harijan women and children paper pickers on the streets, their work is an ordeal. The hours are very long, the physical strain great, and after it all their collection is bought at a low price by a trader who then makes a profit by selling the waste paper to large factories for recycling. Women felt they could form themselves into a co-operative with the support of SEWA, and "Sujata" was registered in 1982.

Although SEWA was successful in petitioning the state government to allow the co-operative to collect waste paper directly from government offices and institutions, the co-operative still has to consistently face confrontations from vested interests. But the women have not given up. They have bought a place to store their waste paper and compete with the traders. They will not sell their waste at throwaway prices!

Handloom Co-operative

Some of the paper pickers, who were migrants from villages in the Mehsana district, Palanpur and Banaskantha, were on the lookout for a different way to make a living. They were weavers, but economic circumstances had forced them to give up their traditional craft and become labourers. One of the weaver women made a request for assistance from SEWA Bank to restart her loom. Other women revealed that they also had looms at home, unused for lack of capital to buy raw material, or had had to sell the looms they once owned.

SEWA identified twenty-four women weavers from among the paper pickers, and they have come together to form a co-operative, which was registered in early 1984. As a co-operative they are entitled to facilities from the state government in the nature of equipment, financial support and marketing opportunities. A training programme was organised at the All India Handicrafts Board Weaver's Service Centre to restore their craft and vocation to them and enhance their skill. SEWA Bank has provided them loans to buy looms and raw materials. The women are enthusiastic and self-confident. They are already looking for a place to build a shed and work collectively, and SEWA is exploring possibilities of getting work space from the Gujarat Industrial Development Corporation. The co-operative has also appealed to the Industries Department to plan for a Weavers Colony near the city.

Safaikam (Cleaning) Co-operative "Saundarya Mandali"

When the National Institute of Design asked SEWA for the services of some women to clean their campus, thirty paper-picker women were organised for "Saundarya Mandali", to give them a different means of employment as well as bargaining power. Their initial contract for three months was extended to one year.

The co-operative is in its fourth year. Women enter into cleaning contracts with private and public institutes, and by putting in three hours of work a day earn at least Rs. 200 ($16) per month. They have gained experience in working together in different places, and have acquired the skills of systematic work in addition to training in a variety of cleaning processes.

* * *

The nine co-operatives of the SEWA Economic Self-Reliance Wing are of basically two types: the co-operatives that sell services and the production-oriented co-operatives. For the former, SEWA helps in finding contracts. But for the latter, unless a marketing infrastructure is developed, the objective of finding alternative employment is not fully achieved.

SEWA Dastkari Bazaar, a unique market system, is now a regular feature of SEWA's programme. Four times a year in different cities, artisans demonstrate their crafts while they are selling their products directly to consumers. The appreciation they get from the consumers far surpasses any other form of motivation; the opportunity for direct contact with the consumers also makes the artisans aware of the expectations, tastes, and reactions of their "market", helping them modify and diversify their skills and products. SEWA co-operatives participate in this and other such exhibitions held in the country and market their products without the exploitative intervention of middlemen.

SEWA also has two shops in Ahmedabad, in Dariyapur and Ellis Bridge corner, serving as marketing outlets for the co-operatives' artisans.

As a result of several years of persistent efforts, a Government of Gujarat Resolution was passed in 1980 to the effect that all establishments under the Government have to buy their goods and services from women's organisations; only when these organisations submit a certificate that the goods and services are unavailable through them can the Government fill its needs from the open market. This has further helped the marketing of the services of co-operatives like "Sujata" and the products of co-operatives like "Baansri". Since the resolution, the "Hariayali" Vegetable Unit has been supplying fruits and vegetables to all government institutions. This has given a large group of vendors a steady income and also saved them from police harassment in the market places.

Efforts are being made to include vegetable growers, who also happen to be women, in the Unit. However, because the urban and rural jurisdictions are administered separately, bringing the two together poses technical difficulties for the Registrar of Co-operatives.

Alongside the marketing facilities, various training programmes in skill-upgrading as mentioned above have been sponsored by SEWA in collaboration with the All India Handicrafts Board Weaver's Service Centre, the National Institute of Design, the State Department of Social Defence and the state government. In addition to traditional areas, women are also learning skills that were hitherto monopolised by men: carpentry, plumbing, domestic wiring, radio repairing, and videotape production.

To keep abreast of modern technology a team of seventeen, consisting of SEWA organisers and a vegetable vendor, a block-printer, a carpenter, cane and bamboo workers, an incense roller and an agricultural worker, was trained in the use of video as a tool of communication. Illiteracy did not interfere with their handling of the sophisticated equipment. A number of videotapes have been made by the participants on various issues including the problems of self-employed women. They have found video an effective medium through which to express themselves and make themselves visible. The team of producers calls their unit Video SEWA.

Unionising with SEWA is a process of social awakening and development for the working sisters, the SEWA organisers, the labour officers and the employers. As most of the occupations in India are caste based, SEWA's membership similarly reflects the divisions of a caste-ridden society.

However, in SEWA the emphasis is on economic activities; there is an unwritten rule that members do not talk about husbands and children, and because SEWA is a labour union, each member should realise herself as a "worker". With this common self-perception, the SEWA members gradually begin to forget their distances for at least a while and to support one another. It has often happened, for example, that when one occupation (caste) has gone on strike, another occupation (caste) has provided food supplies to the strikers and taken care of their children. In this way SEWA promotes integration and becomes a melting pot of all castes and religions. Joining SEWA, getting together with other sisters, learning the skills of dealing with formal organisations, meeting employers as equals, finding out their legal rights, acting to raise their wages, are usually all entirely new experiences for the women, and result in their taking new, assertive leadership roles.

At the same time the process is a moulding experience for the organisers. They understand their working sisters better and grow closer to them. They, too, face opposition and resistance and have to show personal qualities of courage and persistence. The labour officers come to realise that there is a whole population of workers who have been left out of the labour laws, or for whom the laws are not being implemented, and after their experience with SEWA they are in at least some cases more attentive to the problems of these workers, more helpful in working on solutions. The employers as well are beginning to understand that the working sisters must be treated with respect: their contribution has to be recognised, as does the fact that each sister is not alone but part of an organisation which will defend her.

The SEWA Economic Self-Reliance Wing sees itself as a stepping stone which the women can use to become self-sufficient, to break the vicious circle of debt and dependence on middlemen and traders. Through participation in the economic units the women have gained confidence in entering into non-traditional occupations and activities. Women who have never before sold to the public work in SEWA shops, women go directly to the mills to buy *chindi* and to hospitals, jails, and other institutions to take orders; home-based workers, who are most accustomed to producing for an owner, are introduced to the idea of self-managed production involving all steps of the process, from acquiring raw materials to the final sale. These are small but important steps in changing women's attitudes, so that they are able to take more control of their working environments and to strive for improved working conditions and higher earnings.

However, the greatest change has come in the attitude of the women. For home-based producers in particular, self-managed production involving all steps of the process, from acquiring raw materials to the final sale, is a totally novel idea; they are most accustomed to producing for an owner. At first it was difficult for them to define themselves in relation to SEWA as anything but "labourer". After working for a while they would say, "We are neither owners nor labourers; we are somewhere in between." But now, after time and struggle, they believe, "This is our own production unit." The workers' hope that the production units become registered co-operatives with the women from the community as the share-holders, directors, managers, and workers is being realised. Now their efforts and SEWA's are geared to making these co-operatives a viable part of the economy.

So, this is how in SEWA we try to organise ourselves for self-reliance, building on our existing skills, experiences, and capacity. The struggle to claim our rightful economic place and then move forward in the national economy has only just begun. As prices rise, as new technology is introduced, as urbanisation increases, more and more working sisters all over the country will come under attack. We hope the sisters will be able to organise to present a united front for defence.

From Cradle to Grave

JOAN LESTOR

Joan Lestor has a history of involvement with children, race relations, and the Third World. She has travelled extensively, particularly in Africa and the West Indies, and knows these areas well. As an activist, she is well known for her involvement in the Anti-Apartheid Movement, and has represented the UK at the Zimbabwe independence elections.

All her adult life, Joan Lestor has campaigned for a better deal for the "under fives" and for improved trade and relations with the Third World. She recently attended the Harare Conference on the Repression and Torture of Children Under Apartheid and is currently chairperson of the UK branch of Defence for Children International.

The late President Samora Machel of Mozambique often referred to his country's children as "the flowers that never wither". His optimism for the future generations of Mozambicans is echoed in all communities throughout the world. The grim reality today is that in Mozambique and in many other nations children are bearing the brunt of the crisis of poverty, famine and war.

According to the *1988 State of the World's Children Report*, published by the United Nations Children's Fund, one death in every three in the world is the death of a child under the age of five. Each week that goes by, more than a quarter of a million young children are dying in a "silent emergency" of disease and malnutrition. Many of the survivors, says UNICEF, "live on with ill health and poor growth, unable today to develop their full mental and physical potential, unable tomorrow to fully contribute to the families they will have or the communities in which they will live".

Last year some 14 million children under the age of five in developing countries died. The major causes of this stunning death toll are diarrhoea, diseases such as measles, tetanus, whooping cough and polio, acute respiratory infections and undernutrition. But it is known that the threat posed by disease and malnutrition can be defeated. Using low-cost health care and providing the knowledge of its use to parents could drastically reduce the number of child deaths. UNICEF estimates that today's carnage of a quarter of a million child deaths each

169

week could be reduced by at least 50%, given adequate resources and the political will to make child survival the priority of the international community.

Much has already been achieved to reduce child deaths. Not only the rate but also the number of child deaths has fallen dramatically. In 1950, for example, the annual number of deaths under the age of five was 25 million. By 1980, the figure was down to 16 million – despite an increase in the number of births. Today the promotion of low-cost health care, such as immunisation and oral therapies against diarrhoeal disease, is saving another 2 million lives a year.

The revolution in child health care is one of the most remarkable achievements this century. Low-cost techniques now exist which can overcome the major child killers. The figure reproduced opposite illustrates the number of deaths caused and the health care solutions available.

Probably the most extraordinary breakthrough is oral rehydration therapy which is the name given to a sugar, salt and water solution which prevents loss of body fluids during episodes of diarrhoea. Some 4 million children die each year from the effects of diarrhoea which is the leading cause of child death. Using specially formulated oral rehydration salts, which cost just a few pence, about 70% of these children's lives could be saved.

Similarly there have been great steps forward in immunisation against the major childhood diseases. In the 1980s just three vaccine-preventable infections – measles, whooping cough and tetanus – have killed approximately 25 million young children; more than the whole under-five population of Western Europe. However, immunisation has gathered momentum with coverage extending from less than 10% to about 50% of the developing world's children in the 1980s. As a result vaccines are now estimated to be saving the lives of some 1.4 million children each year.

Fig. 1 Annual under-five deaths, developing countries, 1987*

Deaths in millions (cumulative)

14
13

Diarrhoeal diseases
5 million

(also a major cause
of malnutrition)

Of which approximately 3.5 million were caused by dehydration which could have been prevented or treated by low-cost action using oral rehydration therapy.

12

11

10

9

Malaria
1 million

Can be drastically reduced by low-cost drugs if parents know signs and can get help.

8

Measles
1.9 million

(also a major cause
of malnutrition)

Can be prevented by one vaccination, but it is essential to take the child at the right time – as soon as possible after the age of nine months.

7

6

Acute respiratory
infections
2.9 million

0.6 million whooping cough deaths can be prevented by a full course of DPT vaccine – most of the rest can be prevented by low-cost antibiotics if parents know danger signs and can get help.

5

4

3

Tetanus
0.8 million

Neonatal tetanus kills 0.8 million. Can be prevented by immunization of mother-to-be.

2

Other
2.4 million

Many of which can be avoided by prenatal care, breast-feeding and nutrition education.

1

0

Of the 14 million child deaths each year approximately 10 million are from only four major causes and all are now susceptible to effective low-cost actions by well-informed and well-supported parents.

* For the purposes of this chart, one cause of death has been allocated for each child death when, in fact, children die of multiple causes and malnutrition is a contributory cause in approximately one third of all child deaths.
Source: WHO and UNICEF estimates.

Illustrating this progress has been the dramatic increase in vaccine usage. The worldwide supply of vaccines supplied by UNICEF has increased fourfold between 1982 and 1986. Through the United Nations, the international community has set the target of immunising the majority of children by 1990. But what of the costs of such a target? It is estimated that the cost of immunisation in the developing world is about $500 million each year; the same as the cost of ten advanced F14 Fighter Aircraft.

Sometimes it is argued that fewer child deaths will provoke population pressures. But the evidence suggests the opposite. According to UNICEF, "the pattern of demographic change in all nations shows that there has never been a steep and sustained fall in child births which has not been preceded by a steep and sustained fall in child deaths."

Not surprisingly, families tend to have fewer children when they become more confident that their existing children will survive. Parents will then have only the number of children they want and not anticipate expected deaths with extra births. Therefore, some of the methods to ensure child survival also directly contribute to a reduction in birth rates.

Breast feeding and child spacing, for example, both tend to promote child health and reduce pregnancy rates. Breast feeding acts as a natural contraceptive, helping to delay the return of ovulation and hence the chance of pregnancy. Spacing births obviously decreases population levels whilst being one of the most important factors in improving both the health of the mother and the child.

The experience of the last few decades has been one of major progress. Samora Machel's optimism about the children of Mozambique is warranted. But too often Malthusian despair based on ignorance of the facts, prevents the mobilisation of people and resources that is necessary to offer children a better chance in life; 38,000 young children are dying every day because of common infections and poor nutritional health. At least half these deaths are preventable today but the waste of life and opportunity will continue unless child survival and the defeat of poverty become accepted as the political challenge of the 1990s and beyond.

The 1980s: The Impact of Recession

Rather than accept the challenge to improve child welfare, the 1980s have moved away from the struggle against poverty. For the developing world, recession has dominated the decade and the process of long-term development has been stalled. Most dramatically, the Third World is suffering from the debt crisis. A financial famine has swept through Africa and Latin America. "Must we starve our children to pay our debts?" is the stark question posed by former President Julius Nyerere of Tanzania.

There can be no real prospect of an improvement in child welfare if the Third World debt burden is not lifted. Indeed, there is mounting evidence that presently declining infant mortality rates will rise again. The net flow of finance is now heavily from the poor countries to the rich nations of the world. The repayment of debt and interest now substantially exceeds new flows of aid and credit. Today some $27 billion dollars is being transferred to the industrialised countries from the Third World. As recently as 1981 the net flow was over $40 billion, but in the opposite direction: to the benefit of developing countries. This sudden reversal is strangling the fragile economies of Africa and Latin America.

The debt crisis has been caused by the world recession and record interest charges combined with depressed commodity prices. The loss of earnings on major exports such as copper, rubber, tin, sugar and other primary products has devastated the finances of many countries.

As a result, the levels of economic growth and income per head have slumped. Rising unemployment and cuts in social expenditure have been inevitable. Often women and children have been the hardest hit by recession.

Not all nations have suffered equally. Several of the most populous nations of Asia, such as India and China, have been able to insulate themselves from the worst of the recession. But for many countries, especially in Africa and Latin America, the 1980s have been a cruel decade. International economic forces, mostly beyond these countries' control, have played havoc with their prospects for development. The combination of growing debt and falling incomes has bankrupted many nations and stalled their economic progress.

As a result income per head has fallen by 0.6% each year from 1980 to 1985 in developing countries as a whole. It fell in seventeen out of twenty-three countries in Latin America and in twenty-four out of thirty-two countries in sub-Saharan Africa. Overall, income per head fell by 9% in Latin America and by 15% in sub-Saharan Africa.

No set of statistics can adequately convey the human misery caused by such poor economic performance. The first to suffer are the children. In the sub-Saharan, for example, the number of severely hungry and malnourished children has risen by 25% in the past ten years. This rapid physical decline of children highlights the fact that tens of millions of human beings are living literally on the margin of life.

The recession has provoked many nations to adopt drastic reforms of their domestic economies. With import bills and debt repayments heavily outweighing export earnings, aid and bank loans, many countries have faced major balance of payments difficulties. Often, they have accepted policy reform gain loans from the International Monetary Fund (IMF) with stringent conditions attached, that all too often provoke austerity rather than economic growth. When such economic strains become unsustainable, policy reforms are inevitable. Such reforms are termed "adjustment policies" and now dominate the daily lives of millions of Third World people.

Some seventy nations have undertaken policy reform since 1980. A typical reform package aims to reduce balance of payments deficits, curtail "non-essential" imports, ensure debt and interest payments are made and lay foundations for future economic growth. Such measures place a heavy burden on the poor, especially women and children. Increased food prices, reduced wages and cuts in public spending such as health care, frequently harm the welfare of the most vulnerable groups.

A recent study by Richard Jolly, Andrea Cornia and Frances Stewart, *Adjustment With a Human Face* (published by Oxford University Press for UNICEF) argues that it is neither inevitable nor necessary to harm the poor and vulnerable, especially children, during periods of economic hardship such as those currently facing many countries in Africa and Latin America. Their report shows how policies to protect the poor can be developed and heavily criticises the current approach to "adjustment".

Based on studies of ten countries in Latin America, Africa and Asia, Jolly et al show that "the standard of health and education services is declining in many countries" and that "deteriorating health and nutrition is widespread" among the young children of Africa and Latin America. The report shows that malnutrition, low birth weights and child deaths are on the increase among the poor of such countries as Barbados, Belize, Bolivia, Brazil, Chile, Jamaica, the Philippines, Uruguay and several African nations where the years of recession have been aggravated by recent drought.

Adjustment with a Human Face proposes an alternative approach. Governments and international agencies such as the IMF and the World Bank must consciously adopt policies which protect and even improve the wellbeing of the poorest during their period of hardship. A more human-centred approach will aim to restore economic growth but additionally guarantee the prospects of the poor through a range of measures to help low-income groups and especially nursing mothers and children. The existing achievements in child survival already mentioned, such as immunisation and oral rehydration therapy, provide examples of effective, and inexpensive policies to help the poor.

But it must be recognised that developing nations will only be able to devote substantial resources to shield the poor from austerity if the world economic environment is more favourable to the weaker countries. More resources will be a prerequisite of *Adjustment with a Human Face.* The industrialised countries must support a range of policy changes to help the Third World. An increase in the prices of Third World primary commodities to achieve fairer international trade will be required; more generous levels of official overseas aid must be provided; the relaxation of debt repayment schedules and, especially in Africa, complete debt forgiveness would be especially valuable to restore the process of development.

This plea for a more equitable approach to economic reform is based not just on a moral appeal. As Richard Jolly explains, "to miss out the human dimension of adjustment is an economic error of the most fundamental sort. Much evidence already exists of the economic returns to investment in human resources. To fail to protect young children at the critical stages of their growth is to wreak lasting damage on a whole generation, the results of which may well have effects on economic development and welfare for the decades ahead."

Some countries have begun to tackle the issues of adjustment and the poor. Ghana, for example, has undertaken a major programme of economic reform with loans from the IMF and the World Bank. However, the Ghanaian Government has not ignored the impact of policy reform on the poor. With help from UNICEF and other specialised agencies a Programme of Action to Mitigate the Social Consequences of Adjustment (PAMSCAD) has been developed. The programme consists of a range of projects worth $84 million designed to assist the poorest groups. But most importantly, Ghana's poverty programme depends for its success on additional aid from the industrialised countries.

For developed and developing countries alike the crux of the matter lies in political priorities. All governments can choose to make child welfare and poverty alleviation a central object of policy. Without the political will to reverse the lost ground in the 1980s the prospects for the poor, especially women and children, remain grim.

For even in recession, when expenditure cuts are inevitable, choices can be made by the political leadership of developing nations. Should the armaments budget or health be hit? Subsidies to a national airline which caters for 2% of the population or a food programme providing a lifeline to the poorest 20%? Even within the health sector choices can be made between rural health clinics and prestige urban hospitals, or in education, between village primary schools and a city university.

Choices can also be made by the governments of the industrialised countries. The rich nation members of the Organisation of Economic Co-operation and Development (OECD) have a decisive influence over the world economy and, hence, over the prospects for the Third World.

Adjustments in trade, financial and aid policies by the OECD nations, for better or worse, shape the economic environment of the developing countries. The price we pay for commodities; the trade restrictions we impose; the interest charges we demand are all crucial facts of economic life for the poorer nations. The prices of copper or tea may seem remote to issues of child survival. But today they critically determine the scope for Third World governments to promote child welfare.

The industrialised countries, therefore, have a special role and responsibility towards the developing countries. Our nations effectively control the decisions of the international economy and of its major institutions such as the IMF and the World Bank. If the world community wants to take positive steps to guarantee child survival, then the rich countries can make that choice and provide the resources required.

For many of the poorest debtor countries, especially in sub-Saharan Africa, much greater levels of official development assistance are urgently needed. But the aid-giving performance of the OECD nations is woefully inadequate. The level of aid is still 50% below the United Nations agreed target of 0.7% of Gross National Product. Future prospects for growth in aid spending remain poor. The UN target remains elusive for all but a handful of countries (Norway, Holland, Sweden, and Denmark) that have reached the 0.7% figure.

The British Government's aid figure is amongst the most dismal, having been subjected to brutal cuts under Mrs Thatcher's Tory administration. In 1979, the Labour Government left office with a level of aid spending of 0.52% of GNP. The aid budget was increasing and we were the leading aid-giving nation of the top seven OECD nations. Today our performance has slumped to a mere 0.32% of GNP, a level of aid well below the OECD average. Such cuts in aid represent a callous indifference to the plight of children in the Third World.

Indeed, the cuts have borne heavily on UNICEF, the specialised agency of the United Nations that is mandated to work to promote child welfare. If the UK had maintained in real terms the level of its contribution to UNICEF achieved in 1979, the agency would have gained an additional £37 million. But instead the Tory Government substantially reduced the UK share of UNICEF's budget. The lost £37 million would have been sufficient to cover the cost of immunisation for about 7 million children.

It is hard to understand how any government can justify such severe cuts in aid spending. They represent exactly the wrong signal to the international community: the dismissal of child welfare as a key priority for governments and all the people throughout the world. Truly the cruellest cut of all.

Alongside increases in overseas aid, steps must urgently be taken to alleviate the debt burdens of the Third World. The last Labour Government began to tackle this issue in 1978. We agreed to turn all previous aid loans into outright grants for the poorest countries. Their aid debts were effectively written off. Fortunately the Tory Government was unable to renege on this agreement. Indeed, they have recently championed the scheme as an example of their generosity to the debtor nations of Africa!

Rather than borrow Labour policies from the late 1970s, a British government of the late 1980s should take fresh initiatives to tackle the debt crisis. For example, large debts have now accumulated to the international agencies such as the World Bank. Imaginative proposals are required to write off, reschedule and refinance some of these debts. Similarly, commercial bank debt has reached record levels in Latin America and will require much longer-term rescheduling of payments with lower interest charges, combined with some proportion of debt write-off. These are the kinds of solutions that are required to restore the social and economic progress that developing countries so desperately need.

Advocates of Democratic Socialism, who recognise the validity of the One World concept, will need little persuasion for the need to take action. In the hard-headed world of international finance the arguments are still to be won. Perhaps when the world's finance ministers gather at the

IMF they should ask these simple questions, posed by Richard Jolly: "How many of us would countenance rising malnutrition among our own children, without taking or demanding drastic remedial action? How many of us would be willing to accept for our own families a period of austerity so severe as to cause rising malnutrition among our own children? If our personal answers are so clear, can we not work together in an urgent search for alternatives internationally and nationally?"

In a world that tolerates annual world military expenditure of over $900 million, it is easy to understand, if not accept, how child welfare can be overlooked. Arms spending has continued to escalate in both industrialised and developing countries to the extent that the rich countries are now spending more than twenty times as much on the military as on development aid. Meanwhile the developing world spends twice as much on arms as on the health of its children. In total, world military expenditure amounts to more than the entire income of 1,500 million people living in the poorest fifty countries in the world.

It is hardly surprising, therefore, that the 1980s are not just a decade of recession but also a period in which children increasingly suffer from the impact of conflict and war. Civil strife in many parts of Africa, in Central America and the Middle East tear communities apart and make children innocent victims. As one aid worker from the Lebanon commented recently "the real hostages in Beirut are the children".

The impact of war on children is nowhere more acute than in southern Africa. This strife-torn region must cope with its own development under the threat of drought, debt and destabilisation. Children in southern Africa are paying a heavy price for living on the frontline.

Some 15 million children live on the borders of apartheid in the nine independent states of southern Africa. These countries – Angola, Botswana, Lesotho, Malawi,

Mozambique, Swaziland, Tanzania, Zambia and Zimbabwe – are all subject either directly or indirectly to South Africa's military and economic influence. The antagonism, provoked by the apartheid system, towards the frontline states is increasingly explicit. Using both direct military intervention, support for rebel surrogates and economic warfare, South Africa systematically destabilises the entire region.

In the most severely affected countries, economic disruption and military activities have increased child death rates by an estimated 75%. As a result, Mozambique and Angola are suffering the highest child death rates in the world. Both these countries have faced direct military assault by South African forces and civil war with Pretoria-backed rebel forces.

Mozambique's war against the so-called "Renamo" guerrillas has caused, for example, widespread destruction of health and education facilities in the country. Since 1982, 585 health posts and health centres (almost half of the total) have been destroyed. More than a third of all schools have been ruined or abandoned, leaving 500,000 primary-school children without school facilities.

The rebels have deliberately targeted health centres and workers. Brutal acts of terrorism have occurred, all designed to destroy rural life. The Mozambique Government has suffered costs of about $5.5 billion in war damage. Crucial services in health care for women and children have been disrupted. Vaccination programmes have been halted with the result that preventable diseases are claiming a growing toll of young Mozambican lives.

According to UNICEF, by 1986 a total of 140,000 children in Angola and Mozambique had lost their lives as a direct consequence of war and destabilisation. Angola has also suffered severe damage to its health care services. As a result of the war with UNITA forces (again supported by South Africa) health services have declined by 30%. The total cost of the war in Angola is estimated at $17 billion.

Every four minutes an Angolan or Mozambican child dies. Over the period 1980 to 1986 the total of war-related deaths of infants and children under five in these two countries alone was just over half a million.

Southern Africa urgently needs peace and an end to apartheid. In the meantime we can extend our solidarity to the frontline states. Countries like Mozambique urgently need finance, food, drugs, transport and water supplies. Through voluntary agencies or special appeals, funds can be channelled now to ensure that the children of Mozambique remain, in Samora Machel's words, "the flowers that never wither".

In South Africa itself, children have become engaged in the struggle against apartheid. Ever since the Soweto revolt in 1976, black children and students have been playing a central role in the resistance against white domination. They have fought against racist education and to democratise their divided society.

Increasingly, however, the apartheid system has directed repressive measures against black children. The Declaration of a State of Emergency in June 1986 resulted in the detention of over 30,000 people, of whom at least 10,000 were children. Between 1984 and 1986 over 300 children were killed by South African police gunfire and 1,000 were wounded.

Held in Zimbabwe in September 1987, the Harare Conference on Children, Repression and the Law in Apartheid South Africa documented South Africa's brutality towards children. The conference heard moving testimony from South African children about their own experiences of torture and detention. In a declaration it urged lawyers, medical practitioners, social and religious workers, and all others whose work involves special responsibilities for children to play a part in the struggle to protect the children of South Africa and free them from apartheid. Building such anti-apartheid alliances will be even more important following the banning in late February 1988 of the United Democratic Front.

Of course the situation of children in South Africa is extreme and apartheid is a uniquely repressive system. But children throughout the world are facing a struggle for recognition; a positive demand for rights. In such a brief survey of child welfare issues, this chapter inevitably leaves out many pressing concerns: the problems of child labour, child abuse and sexual exploitation.

These questions are of growing significance and require urgent action by the international community. The burgeoning number of street children, for example, puts millions at risk of the worst forms of child exploitation. The rapid growth of urban populations in cities throughout the Third World has produced a similar increase in the number of children who live as street urchins or *gamins*. In Latin America there are an estimated 40 million such children living a life of extreme neglect and poverty. Their existence there and elsewhere is symbolic of society's neglect.

At the very least the international community must consciously recognise the plight of such children. Governments need to accept responsibilities and children must be granted their rights. Modest progress is being made on developing a framework for children's rights. Since 1979, a working group of the United Nations Commission on Human Rights has been drafting the text of a Convention on the Rights of a Child. Hopefully this task may well be completed for adoption at the United Nations in September 1989, (a symbolic year that marks the thirtieth anniversary of the Declaration of the Rights of the Child and the tenth anniversary of the International Year of the Child).

The draft convention includes thirty-five articles covering civil, political, economic, social and cultural rights. The rights it sets out are based on three principles: that children need special safeguards beyond those provided to adults; that the best environment for a child's survival and development is within the family; and that governments and the adult world should act in the best interest of children.

The articles of the convention provide "basic needs" rights such as adequate food, water, health care and shelter; and "protective" rights against abuse, neglect and exploitation. Governments that formally accept and sign the convention will have the responsibility of meeting these provisions and adapting their own domestic laws and regulations.

Inevitably international codes, such as the proposed convention, have limited legal force. Nevertheless, they do provide a reference point from which to judge the performance of nations throughout the world. Such standard-setting is of great significance and provides a tool for examination and campaigning. But no convention or other legal code can guarantee children's rights. Only the political will of people and their governments can safeguard child welfare.

Recent experience suggests that little more than lip service will be paid to the lofty aims of the UN Convention. Mobilisation of political will, the traditional task of the Labour Movement in Britain and abroad is required to advance the cause of children's rights. Our concern is not abstract, nor is it sentimental. Progress and development in our One World depends on investment in people. And children, the wealth creators of future generations, are the best investment of all.

The Frontline States of Southern Africa

MARGARET LING

Margaret Ling is a member of the national executive committee of the Anti-Apartheid Movement and Editor of its newspaper, *Anti-Apartheid News*. She is a founder member and director of AA Enterprises, a workers' co-operative trading in support of the Anti-Apartheid Movement and the frontline states of Southern Africa. She is an executive member of the Britain-Zimbabwe Society and has extensive contacts in that country, particularly with the collective co-operative movement. Margaret Ling lives and works in London.

Introduction

> We in Africa have to maintain the struggle for justice,
> for equality and for freedom within the independent
> countries of our continent . . . As we succeed in these
> endeavours, we do, ourselves, inflict defeats upon
> apartheid. (Julius Nyerere, former President of Tan-
> zania, December 1987)

The six frontline states of southern Africa, Angola, Botswana, Mozambique, Tanzania, Zambia and Zimbabwe,
together with the neighbouring states of Lesotho and
Swaziland, face a peculiarly unjust irony. They are fighting one of the twentieth century's most misrepresented
and under-reported wars, against a regime which the
world at large detests and condemns.

It is hard to find a single government which has
anything but harsh words for South Africa's apartheid
policies. Mrs Thatcher herself has declared that she
deplores apartheid and finds it repulsive. Yet day after
day, week after week, little or no effective action is taken
to stop the South African regime from exporting terror
and death to the people of the neighbouring states, and
laying waste thousands of square miles of otherwise
fertile and prosperous countryside.

The catalogue of suffering in the frontline states of
southern Africa is lengthy and grim. Since 1980, at least
three quarters of a million children and adults are esti-

mated to have died as a result of South Africa's armed incursions. In Angola alone, at least 25,000 people have been disabled, probably the highest per capita rate in the world. The damage caused to all the six countries amounts to at least US $25 billion over the same period, while they have been obliged to spend up to half of their national budgets defending themselves from continuing attack. More than 2 million people have been displaced from their homes and turned into destitute wanderers in their own land. The child mortality rate has risen remorselessly and the prospects for the future are bleak. And yet this is a region rich in natural and human resources and potentially able to help shift the economy of the African continent as a whole from dependence to self-sufficiency. Why is this happening and what can be done?

South African Attacks

South Africa's aggression against the frontline and neighbouring states takes many forms and is well described in a number of publications available from the Anti-Apartheid Movement. (See, for example, *Apartheid's Second Front – South Africa's War Against its Neighbours*, by Joseph Hanlon, Penguin Special, 1986; *Destructive Engagement*, edited by David Martin and Phyllis Johnson, Zimbabwe Publishing House, 1986; and issues of *Anti-Apartheid News*.)

Direct and open cross-border violations by South African military forces. These have included aerial bombings against the capitals of Zambia, Botswana, Zimbabwe and Mozambique, and attacks by ground forces ranging in scale from one-off raids to the sustained mass invasion and attempted occupation of large parts of southern Angola. The assault on Angola is doubly illegal in that it is launched by South Africa from illegally occupied Namibia. In February 1988, there were an estimated 9,000 South African troops on Angolan soil. These attacks, "justified" by South Africa on the grounds of "defence", are mounted against countries which have never shown the slightest inclination to violate South African territory, let alone invade.

Direct but clandestine attacks by South African military agents. These include assassinations by various methods, including letter, parcel and car bomb attacks, supposedly directed against exiled members of the liberation movements and sympathisers but in practice causing the death and injury of many totally unconnected residents of the countries concerned; kidnappings and abduction; arson; theft; sabotage operations against economic and military targets; mercenary operations and attempted coups. Such clandestine operations have been mounted by South Africa in countries far beyond the frontline states themselves, including Britain.

Military destabilisation through surrogate forces. The most notorious surrogate forces are the MNR or "Renamo" in Mozambique (originally set up by intelligence agents of the illegal Rhodesian regime, but handed over to South African control after Zimbabwe's independence) and Unita in Angola (led by Jonas Savimbi, who previously co-operated with the Portuguese secret police PIDE and since Angola's independence has worked closely with both the South African regime and the CIA).

South Africa has also been responsible for training and infiltrating armed dissident or bandit elements in Zimbabwe and Zambia and, in the neighbouring state of Lesotho, the forces of the Lesotho Liberation Army (LLA).

South Africa's surrogate forces are responsible for some of the most horrific and cruel forms of terrorist attack in a world grown sadly inured to violence and atrocity. They include the deliberate disablement of the local civilian population through laying landmines, massacres, rape, burning, looting and pillage, and torture and maiming through cutting off ears, lips, noses, breasts and other bodily organs. These bandit groups have no clear political philosophy to offer, beyond causing maximum chaos and destruction of social and economic development programmes such as health services, schools, shops, plantations, factories, warehouses, public transport and communications, and the kidnapping of overseas aid and development workers. One aim is to blackmail the governments of the frontline states into "recognising" the bandits through inclusion in "peace negotiations" whose real purpose is to win credibility for the surrogate's controllers: apartheid South Africa itself.

Direct economic destabilisation. South Africa makes full use of the ties of economic dependence, especially in transport and communications, which the frontline states have inherited from their colonial past. These especially affect landlocked Botswana, Zambia and Zimbabwe, in the past almost totally dependent on South Africa for import and export routes other than by air. Mozambique, Angola and Tanzania, where alternative transport routes were neglected in colonial times or have since been systematically attacked as part of South Africa's destabilisation strategy, are victims in a different but equally damaging way.

The targeting of independent transport routes such as the Beira Corridor (road, rail and oil pipeline) from Zimbabwe through Mozambique, and the Benguela Railway from Zambia and Zaire through Angola, has caused enormous loss of revenue to Angola and Mozambique and reinforced the dependence of other countries on South Africa's own transport and port system. The South African Government has openly boasted that aircraft and equipment, obtained through arms embargo busting deals with Western countries such as the Federal Republic of

Germany and Britain, enable it to attack such far-flung transport links as the Tazara Railway from Zambia through Tanzania as well.

Propaganda and disinformation. South Africa's own powerful state communications network, its control of the press and media through a vast array of repressive laws including its State of Emergency regulations, and the compliant attitude of much of the world's press, enable it to conceal the real source of conflict in southern Africa and to misrepresent and discredit the frontline states.

South Africa has set up special radio stations in the Transvaal and elsewhere to beam disinformation into Angola (Voice of the Black Cockerel, supposedly a Unita station), Mozambique (Voice of Free Africa) and Zimbabwe (Radio Truth). It has showered leaflets and pamphlets on to the civilian populations of the frontline states to persuade them that South African attacks are somehow the "fault" of their own independent governments. And it directs a constant stream of propaganda, distortion and outright lies at the international media.

South Africa's aim internationally is to undermine anti-apartheid solidarity by making it appear that the frontline governments are incapable of running their countries, self-seeking, dishonest and unconcerned about the suffering of their own people. Its own surrogate forces, meanwhile, are presented as independent movements or "pro-Western freedom fighters" fighting "civil wars" in pursuit of democracy in their own countries. In Angola's case in particular, the Angolan people's efforts to defend their sovereignty and independence against apartheid attack are presented in terms of East-West conflict and the supposed territorial ambitions of the Soviet Union.

Unfortunately, much South African propaganda reaches British newspapers, radios and TV screens in virtually undigested form, served up without critical comment or disclaimer to an unsuspecting or uncaring public. The violations of international and humanitarian law at stake are rarely mentioned or explained.

The Lessons of History

The six countries, Angola, Botswana, Mozambique, Tanzania, Zambia and Zimbabwe, are not known as the frontline states solely because they are direct targets for South African attack – so are the neighbouring states of Lesotho and Swaziland. The term "frontline states" also refers to the principled positions which the six have adopted towards the southern African freedom struggle and to the political structures which they have built up to co-ordinate their responses to the apartheid war. All six independent states are united by the conviction that not only they, but Africa as a whole, cannot be truly free until Namibia and South Africa are free and the apartheid system has been finally overthrown.

This conviction reflects the frontline states' own history. All have achieved their political independence after decades, if not centuries, of colonial domination. In the case of Mozambique, Angola and Zimbabwe in particular, that independence was only won after years of bitter conflict and armed struggle by liberation movements whose leaders and members inspired solidarity action all over the world, including Britain.

Tanzania the first of the frontline states to achieve its independence, was a German colony from 1884 to 1914, and later administered by Britain as a United Nations trust territory. Formed by the union in 1964 of Tanganyika (independent since 1961) and the islands of Zanzibar and Pemba, Tanzania has since offered shelter to many exiled African nationalist leaders as well as providing secure rear bases for Frelimo's independence struggle in neighbouring Mozambique. Although geographically far from South Africa, Tanzania has played a vital role in African and international solidarity and is itself far from immune from apartheid attack and destabilisation.

Zambia, the former British colony of Northern Rhodesia, won its independence in 1964 and up to 1980 served as a frontline state for the Zimbabwe liberation struggle, providing shelter and support for thousands of Zimbabwean refugees and exiles. Today it offers rearguard support to both SWAPO of Namibia and the African National Congress of South Africa and chairs the frontline states grouping.

Botswana, formerly Bechuanaland, was one of three British protectorates together with Swaziland and Basutoland, now Lesotho. Like Zambia, it served as a refuge for Zimbabwean exiles and freedom fighters during the struggle against the illegal Smith regime and has long been a sympathetic transit route for South African exiles. Botswana, three quarters surrounded by apartheid rule from the illegally occupied Caprivi Strip of Namibia down to South Africa itself, is in a particularly vulnerable position.

Mozambique won its independence on 25 June 1975 after a decade of armed struggle against Portuguese colonialism. It is all too familiar with the kind of repression and violence endured by black South Africans and Namibians today. It is a little-known fact that 16 June, South African Youth Day and the anniversary of the Soweto uprising in which hundreds of school children and students were murdered by South African police, is also the anniversary of another blood-stained event in Mozambican history. Fifteen years previously, on 16 June 1960, Portuguese colonial forces massacred 600 unarmed Mozambicans protesting against the occupation of their country in

Mueda, Cabo Delgado province, near the border with Tanzania.

Following its own independence, Mozambique provided a vital rear base for the Zimbabwean liberation movement (ZANU), suffering punitive raids by Ian Smith's armed forces as a result as well as the dreadful heritage of the MNR, formed by Smith to destabilise the Frelimo Government.

Angola won its independence on 11 November 1975, wresting its freedom from invading South African and CIA forces bent on preventing the MPLA liberation movement from taking over the country. Ever since then, Angola has been forced to defend itself from South African aggression and invasion launched from the illegally occupied territory of Namibia and backed up by US pressure. Despite its own extreme difficulties, Angola provides shelter for thousands of Namibian refugees and vital rear bases for both the African National Congress and South West Africa People's Organisation.

Zimbabwe, the youngest of the frontline states, achieved independence on 18 April 1980, nearly fifteen years after Ian Smith's Unilateral Declaration of Independence (UDI) from British colonial rule. South African support for the illegal regime, backed up by British unwillingness to take effective measures against white Rhodesian "kith and kin", still could not prevent the liberation movement from eventually winning majority rule.

Since 1980 Zimbabwe has rapidly moved to prominence in African, commonwealth and world affairs, culminating in its hosting of the 1986 Non-Aligned Summit. Its independence also led to the formation of the frontline states grouping itself as a formally constituted entity. Today, the leaders of the six countries meet regularly to co-ordinate policies and practical initiatives.

The victories won by the peoples of Mozambique, Angola and Zimbabwe during the 1970s changed the whole face of southern Africa and were a source of tremendous inspiration to those still fighting for freedom in Namibia and South Africa itself. They brought the prospect of liberation almost within grasp by proving that the vastly superior forces of the colonial and occupying powers *could* be overcome through the will of the people.

Those victories have not brought peace to the frontline states, however. Instead of an opportunity to consolidate their independence and to build a better life for their peoples, they have not had a moment's respite from apartheid attack. But despite the huge price of solidarity, they have never wavered in their commitment to the anti-apartheid cause.

Together with Lesotho, Swaziland and Malawi, the frontline states comprise the nine-nation Southern African Development Co-ordination Conference (SADCC), formed in 1980. The SADCC is a regional grouping established to reduce dependence on apartheid South Africa, to build strong self-reliant economies through mutual self-help and co-operation, and to realise the benefits of large-scale regional co-ordination and planning.

The Frontline States and Sanctions

What needs to be done by the international community to combat apartheid has been made perfectly clear on many occasions by the frontline states. They want the world – and above all, Britain and the other Western nations which have the economic clout to make such action really effective – to impose comprehensive mandatory sanctions against South Africa without any further delay.

Economic sanctions are the international community's long accepted, non-violent means of undermining the apartheid regime's capacity to maintain itself in power, so giving invaluable assistance to those fighting for human rights and democracy within South Africa and Namibia themselves. Above all, an effective arms embargo, including properly enforced bans on the supply of all military-related equipment, expertise and skilled personnel, and strategic materials including oil and fuel supplies, would make it difficult and ultimately impossible for South Africa to carry on attacking the frontline states.

The frontline states do not, as Mrs Thatcher and Pretoria's other allies would like the world to believe, see sanctions as an insurmountable threat to their own economies, but as a vital investment for the future. They have repeatedly said that they are prepared to face any short-term difficulties and hardships that sanctions might bring, for the sake of the much more important goal of bringing apartheid to an end. The economic, political and social costs of defending the frontline states against South African aggression (an estimated US $27.5 billion since 1980 alone) already go far beyond what their hard-pressed economies can afford.

The frontline states are in any case all too familiar with the effects of sanctions, in that South Africa has for many years been applying its own sanctions against them as part of its overall destabilisation strategy and in reprisal for anti-apartheid action from the international community. The frontline states have made clear their view that if the world is really serious about taking action against apartheid, any programme of sanctions needs to be accompanied by effective support to the frontline and neighbouring states to enable them to weather the consequences. Such aid is not an *alternative* to sanctions, as proposed by Mrs Thatcher at the 1987 Vancouver Commonwealth Summit, but a vital complement.

The Frontline States – A Threat to Apartheid?

Why does South Africa put so much effort into attacking the frontline states?

The answer to this question, in terms of the commitment of the frontline states to supporting the Namibian and South African liberation struggles and their repeated calls for international sanctions, may seem obvious. The Pretoria regime hopes through its aggression to demoralise and divide the peoples of the frontline states and to convince them that the effort and sacrifice entailed by their stand are not worthwhile. South Africa sees the frontline states as potentially the weakest links in the international sanctions campaign and intends to use their dependency to undermine any sanctions that are imposed.

But South Africa also attacks the frontline states because their very existence challenges the basic principles of white supremacy. The presence on South Africa's doorstep of independent countries which have won their political freedom through struggle, and which remain determined to reconstruct their societies in their own way despite enormous obstacles and provocation, is anathema to its rulers. The frontline states must be destroyed if Pretoria is to "prove" one of its central arguments: that non-racial democracies can never work in Africa.

The frontline states are well aware of their responsibilities in this regard, not only to their own citizens but to the generations to come. President Eduardo dos Santos of Angola, addressing the Angolan People's Assembly in January 1987, had this to say:

> The fate to which imperialism has relegated the great majority of peoples of the so-called third world is one of sacrifice and struggle for the welfare and freedom of coming generations . . . We accept the fact that the

197

present generation is being sacrificed by history and we do not renounce our responsibilities to build the free and prosperous country of the future.

What is being built up in the frontline states represents something dramatically new and different from what has gone before in southern Africa. The experience and commitment built up through the pre-independence years of struggle have since been put to use in mutual assistance to combat apartheid.

Such solidarity amongst the frontline states exists both at government and grassroots level. Zimbabwe, for example, is heavily committed to defending and supporting the Mozambique Government, both out of self-interest and in recognition of the help which its own people received from the newly independent Frelimo Government in the second half of the 1970s. At grassroots level, a countrywide programme of material aid and solidarity with Mozambique has been developed in Zimbabwe under the auspices of the Zimbabwe Mozambique Friendship Association (ZIMOFA), a non-governmental agency founded by volunteers.

All the frontline states are heavily committed to caring for refugees and exiles from South Africa and Namibia and co-operate for this purpose. The SADCC too, which unlike the European Economic Community does not have an unwieldy central bureaucracy, has led to the growth of a variety of regional groupings and federations representing women, youth, the trade union movement and other interest groups. A new, regional, popular consciousness is emerging based on the central principle of anti-apartheid solidarity.

International Solidarity with the Frontline States

In May 1987, President Joaquim Chissano of Mozambique paid an official visit to Britain at the invitation of

Prime Minister Margaret Thatcher. Despite the clear differences between his own and the British Government's position on sanctions, the Mozambican President stressed his desire for closer links and much deeper understanding between the peoples of the two countries. As he put it:

> We cannot wait for the end of South African destabilisation and for the end of apartheid before developing our co-operation with the west. It is our belief that the seeds of a relationship sown in these difficult times will bear a harvest of firm friendship in the future. (Address to the Royal Institute of International Affairs, London, 7 May 1987.)

President Chissano developed his theme at a solidarity gathering after the close of his official programme, attended by hundreds of friends and supporters of Mozambique from the Mozambique Angola Committee, Anti-Apartheid Movement, trade unions, local authorities, the peace and anti-racist movements, aid agencies, former *co-operantes* and development workers. He declared:

> We cannot praise the Mozambican people for the success of their liberation struggle without mentioning the contribution made by the people of Great Britain. During the liberation war, the British people supported Frelimo, although their governments did not ... Governments come and go, but peoples stay. If friendship between the peoples is ensured, then relations between the two countries will flourish. (AIM, 8 May 1987.)

Grassroots solidarity with the peoples of Mozambique and the other frontline states has a long and honourable history in Britain. Lord Fenner Brockway, the oldest guest, ninety-eight, at the reception at which President Chissano spoke, attended the first Congress of the

Peoples Against Imperialism in Brussels in 1928 and later founded the Movement for Colonial Freedom. The Anti-Apartheid Movement itself was founded in 1959 in response to the South African people's appeal for an international boycott of apartheid. It soon extended its commitment to supporting the struggles in Namibia, against the illegal Smith regime in Rhodesia, and against Portuguese colonialism in Angola and Mozambique.

Today, the frontline states are the natural allies of the Anti-Apartheid Movement in the battle for sanctions against South Africa. They are in the frontline of the apartheid regime's terrorist war. Those in Britain who support the cause of freedom in southern Africa are in the frontline of the battle against collaboration, for it is in Britain, in the corridors of Westminster and the board-rooms of the City of London, that collaboration with Pretoria is most entrenched. British people who care about apartheid have a particular responsibility to protect the interests of the frontline states and to take action on issues which those countries may not be in a position to raise directly themselves.

The position of Mrs Thatcher's Government itself on the issue of the frontline states is an ambivalent and hypocritical one. The Government has been forced by the pressure of events in southern Africa to make some diplomatic overtures towards the frontline states and to give limited material assistance.

These initiatives are not motivated by a genuine desire to fight apartheid in southern Africa. Instead, the British Government hopes to use them to evade pressure to impose sanctions and to strengthen its influence on events in the region in the new circumstances of the struggle. The intention is to put the frontline states in a position where, through indebtedness, they are unable to call clearly for sanctions to be imposed against South Africa.

The British Government is also an active collaborator

in attempts being spearheaded by the Reagan Administration to divide the frontline states on issues such as the supposed "communist threat" to Africa and so to destroy the political unity that has been built up in the 1980s.

The tasks for the Anti-Apartheid Movement in countering such official policy and building real solidarity with the frontline states include:

Publicity and information to expose South Africa's war against the frontline states and to make people aware of their policies towards the liberation struggle and the need for sanctions.

It is also important to publicise the victories that are being won in the frontline states and their achievements in the various fields of economic, social, cultural and political development, despite the very real difficulties they face and the war which they are being forced to fight. The frontline states are far from being helpless victims and the war is certainly not all going South Africa's way.

The frontline states, like other Third World nations, suffer from negative and racist stereotypes perpetuated by much of the Western media coverage, and one of the aims of anti-apartheid information work is to correct these.

Pressure on the British Government through lobbying, protests and demonstrations. As well as endorsing comprehensive mandatory sanctions, a British Government genuinely committed to ending apartheid would also take care to develop an effective policy of aid and support to the frontline states, on terms worked out in full consultation with their governments. The British Government should be encouraging British companies and institutions to be developing other relations with the frontline states as alternatives to their traditional links with apartheid South Africa and on the principles of equal and mutually beneficial partnership.

Support for programmes of material assistance to the frontline states, as requested and formulated by their governments and peoples themselves. Anti-apartheid supporters have developed useful links with the aid and development lobby on the issue of the frontline states, but there is scope for much greater co-operation in this respect. The Anti-Apartheid Movement is also committed to publicising and supporting the AFRICA Fund, launched by the Non-Aligned Movement in 1986 to give emergency and solidarity help to the frontline states and the liberation movements.

Support for alternative trade with the frontline states, by buying and publicising their products and pressurising companies and organisations to develop new economic relations. Such trade may be small in economic terms but it can be an important way of raising the profile of the frontline states and increasing public awareness of their situation and what they have to offer.

Looking to the future. Above all, the Anti-Apartheid Movement sees the frontline states as the logical alternative to apartheid. Mrs Thatcher is fond of presenting herself and her policies as radical and forward-looking, and those of her opponents as old-fashioned. But in relation to one of the most important international issues in the world today – southern Africa – the rest of the world sees her siding with a backward-looking, antiquated regime facing an irreversible and deepening crisis.

Mrs Thatcher is also fond of presenting the alternatives to apartheid as threats to the living standards of British people, using the argument that sanctions will mean the loss of thousands of British jobs. Her argument fails to take into account the potential that the overthrow of apartheid has for creating new jobs by opening up new and mutually beneficial trade and economic relations with the frontline states.

At present all the human and economic resources of

the frontline states are locked up in fighting a senseless and destructive war. When their resources are at last freed for the development of the region, there will be significant repercussions throughout the rest of the world.

Southern Africa is one of the richest and most powerful regions in the southern hemisphere and so the overthrow of the present ruling minority in Pretoria will decisively affect the balance of power between North and South. While this prospect frightens those with vested economic interests in the present system, it has exciting implications for others.

One thing is clear: apartheid cannot survive. The best interests of the British people lie in building links with the free and independent countries of Africa rather than perpetuating existing alliances with racism and reaction. The frontline states are part of that future; apartheid belongs to the past.

South Africa's War Against Children

FRANK CHIKANE

Frank Chikane was born thirty-seven years ago in Orlando East, Johannesburg. He went to the University of the North at Pietersburg where he became a member of the Student Christian Movement. In early 1975, he taught mathematics and physics at Naledi High School and later worked as an evangelist and a pastor in the Apostolic Faith Mission Church.

On 6 June 1977 he was first arrested and tortured, and subsequently arrested and detained without charge four times. He was charged with high treason in 1985 and acquitted after spending almost a year in custody. On his release his house was fire-bombed and he has received death-threats.

He was made General Secretary of the South African Council of Churches in 1987. In April 1988 he publically challenged Mr. P.W. Botha's attack on Archbishop Tutu, and has himself been repeatedly attacked on South African state television. He is seen today as one of South Africa's outstanding Christian leaders.

I am going to concentrate on the context of the present war against the voteless majority in South Africa. To understand the form this war is taking today and the nature of the crisis we are facing we need to trace its origin over the last decade or so of struggle in the country.

I propose to briefly outline the background to the crisis of apartheid and white domination which necessitated a change in government strategy in the late seventies. I am going to argue that this shift did not help the apartheid regime but has instead deepened the crisis and contradictions within the system. This discussion will lead us to the two states of emergency in 1985 and 1986 up to the present day, during which period our children have been badly brutalized.

Background Events Leading to South Africa's Use of the Repressive State Apparatus

The independence of Mozambique and Angola in 1975 altered the balance of forces in the southern African region. It broke the so-called *cordon sanitaire* of white-ruled colonies which gave the apartheid regime the security and confidence to suppress indefinitely the political aspirations of the black majority in the country. The fall of the Portuguese colonies brought the battle front against colonial and neo-colonial rule closer to the heartland of white oppression and exploitation.

This created security problems for South Africa. The 1976 Soweto uprising followed by the November 1977 United Nations Security Council resolution on mandatory arms embargo against South Africa; the guerilla actions of the African National Congress (ANC), which were fuelled by the Soweto uprising; the economic decline from 1974 up to 1978; the substantial outflow of foreign capital; all these deepened the crisis of the regime. White hegemony was clearly under siege.

In response to this crisis the apartheid regime produced the 1977 Defence White Paper which laid the basis for P. W. Botha's belief in a total onslaught on South Africa from beyond its borders. This "total onslaught" needed a "total national strategy". The "total onslaught" which South Africa was facing was articulated as a communist plot. The analyst Joseph Hanlon presents this view of South Africa as follows:

> "The concept of 'total onslaught' equates the 'red peril' with the 'black peril' and defence of apartheid with defence of Western Christian values." (*Beggar your Neighbour. Apartheid Powers in Southern Africa*, Joseph Hanlon, London: CIIR, 1986, p.7.)

Hanlon says that this formulation has two advantages for white South Africa. Firstly, it dismisses all criticism of apartheid as Communist. Secondly, it creates a condition which makes both white South Africans and the West see South Africa as the last bastion against Communism, the protector of Western Christian values. It creates a serious contradiction for the West: making it feel that by attacking apartheid, it is in fact helping the Soviet Union.

The "total strategy" to counter this "total onslaught" consisted, amongst other elements, of the following:

1. The need to forge some kind of national unity government to defend white rule. (The present tricameral system developed from the need of the racist

regime to draw the so-called Indian and coloured populations in South Africa and some middle-class black Africans into a junior partnership with the white minority against the black majority. This was an attempt to pit one group of people against the other.)

2. Repression of all anti-apartheid activists and those who resist this system.

3. The imposition of South African hegemony over the whole southern African region to silence those opposed to apartheid and to neutralise mainly the (ANC) guerrilla warfare against South Africa. This would consist of a combination of diplomatic/political, economic and military strategies. The 1977 Defence White Paper identified the need to maintain a balance relative to all southern African states and also called for economic action to promote political and economic collaboration amongst the states in Southern Africa. This proposed collaboration was later called the Constellation of Southern African States (CONSAS).

The total strategy, therefore, was aimed at establishing South Africa's position as a "regional power" and establishing a "constellation of states" under its tutelage. This would develop a "common approach" on both the security and economic fronts against what was called the expanding Communist influence of the region.

The third leg of this total strategy was aborted by the independence of Zimbabwe and by the formation of the Southern African Development Co-ordination Conference (SADCC), dashing the hope of forming CONSAS.

To understand the context of the war in South Africa we need, therefore, to look at the first two legs of the total strategy, i.e., *reform of government and repression*. It is now a matter of history that the oppressed masses of South Africa saw through the fraud of these reforms. They organised against them and floored them.

The state then resorted to the second leg of the total strategy, i.e., *repression*. The army and the police occupied the townships. Thousands of our people were killed; many thousands were detained; many of them tortured. And all this was directed mainly against young people under the age of twenty-five. Many of these were children under the age of eighteen. The vicious attacks against the people by the state only served to increase their militancy and anger particularly in the young people.

At best, the reform strategies forced people to mobilise and organise against the subtle attempt to further entrench apartheid and maintain white domination. This campaign, led mainly by the United Democratic Front (UDF), galvanised the masses and transformed the face of politics in South Africa.

The political complexion of this country was rapidly transformed as mass organisation spread like a *veldfire*. Throughout the country, from the smallest village to the largest city, the people organised themselves into democratic structures which expressed their needs and aspirations. These structures (street committees, education committees, people's courts, etc.) were declared subversive by the regime because they stood opposed to government apartheid structures.

The arrogance of ignoring the people's rejection of the tri-cameral system, or ignoring the aspirations of the people by imposing the new structures of oppression (after the so-called coloured and Indian elections of August 1984) created an explosive situation which ignited in the Vaal in September 1984. This event sparked off a wave of uprisings around the country, leaving the imposed black local authorities in shambles. The police and those perceived as collaborators and informers were forced out of the townships except when they came in on military or security operations.

In short, the people simply refused to collaborate or co-operate with the system in oppressing them. They refused to be governed by the apartheid regime.

War Against the People of South Africa

The state then declared a state of emergency between July 1985 and March 1986 which was reimposed in June 1986 and is still in existence. The South African Defence Force, a machine of war, was sent into the townships, the schools and the villages, in every part of the country.

Soldiers and police, now called "security forces", were indemnified for any act of violence committed against the local population. They both had unlimited powers to detain, raid and search; break up meetings and funerals; set up road blocks; impose curfews and seal off townships or villages to prevent anyone from entering. Even aircraft could be used in security force "operations" for surveillance, dropping propaganda literature as part of a show of force in rent evictions, and for actually diving on demonstrations. Townships were put under spotlights to facilitate operations at night. There were also reports of military units used in Namibian war zones now being deployed in the townships.

During the state of emergency we have seen the brutal murders of our people by South Africa's security forces', vigilantes and hit squads. People have been displaced because of the terror unleashed by the security forces and assassination squads. We have also seen a vicious disinformation campaign which has cost many lives. This is aggravated by restrictions on the free flow of information.

War Against Children

The mobilisation of the army against the black majority showed very clearly that the regime regarded all oppressed people as "insurgents". It was intent on breaking the spirit of resistance which was sweeping the whole country, and hoped to wipe out the forces of national liberation and create a political wasteland which government proxy forces and other co-optable elements would take over. Reports reaching churches and other bodies monitoring repression around the country clearly indicated that after the state of emergency a wide range of people, regardless of their political involvement, were being terrorised by the forces of so-called law and order. What emerges clearly from these reports is that the main target of this terror has been children and adolescents. This is not surprising because since June 16, 1976, these two groups have provided the most militant, energetic and courageous fighters against apartheid. Many of them are driven by sheer hatred of apartheid to engage daily in a battle with the security forces and all those they regard as enforcing apartheid.

The state has therefore concluded that to break the spirit of the community it has to break the spirit of the young: not only those formally involved in the organisations of the democratic movement, but all young people. The state of emergency has therefore seen a general campaign of terror being waged against our young.

Hundreds of reports have reached us of apparently random assault, harassment and the shooting of young people in the streets, at school, on the way to shops, at funerals, at vigils and so on. A pattern has emerged which has repeated itself in every part of the country. The attacks aren't simply the actions of overzealous security forces, but are actually part of a deliberate policy of terrorising the young.

For everyone who thinks that it is an exaggeration to talk of a policy of terror, consider the experience of a fifteen-year-old boy who has never been an activist and whose statement reads as follows:-

212

On a Friday, after school, I was walking with my friend when I saw a Combi containing policemen coming towards us. My friend was scared so he ran away. Six police, two whites and four blacks, got out of the Combi. The white policeman knocked me down with his gun and then three of them took me to the street corner. The other three had started chasing my friend in a Combi but they did not catch him. The white policeman and two black policemen then assaulted me with rubber truncheons. They threatened me with a knife. One of the policemen told me to run so that they could shoot me. The Combi with the other police then came back and they threw me in the Combi. They drove to a schoolyard where they assaulted me again. They hit me with rubber truncheons and sjamboks (whips). Then they blindfolded me with a greasy cloth and tied my hands behind my back with my belt.

They put me against a wall and said they were going to shoot me. People had come into the schoolyard and when they saw me against the wall, they started screaming. The police then took the blindfold away and showed me a tyre which they said they were going to put on me and then set me alight. A black policeman said that they had been sent from Port Elizabeth to kill people and that I would be an example for them. But the white policeman said they must stop because the other people in the schoolyard had taken the car registration number. Then they took me to a police station and asked the police there to detain me for "suspected car theft". Three days later I was released without being charged for anything.' (Abanawana Bazabalaza, DPSC memo, p. 31.)

To intimidate and demoralise the young, particularly school kids, the police introduced curfews, door-to-door raids, shows of force at funerals and meetings. Our children came under heavy attack in schools. At one stage during the emergency, schools were occupied by the security forces. School children reported that they were terrorised by the security forces. Soldiers and police interfered in the classes, attacked and shot children in the school grounds, whipped them back into their classrooms, etc. A teacher from Tumahole on the Orange Free State said in a sworn affidavit:

Since the reopening of the school term on the 14 July 1986, members of the S. A. Police and council police have been on the school premises [sic] at all times. For me, as a teacher, the very presence of security forces disrupts the teaching programme. My students often ask me why these police are always around, but because of the warnings from the principal I was unable to discuss even these problems with the students in my class . . . During breaktime the security forces bar the gate leading onto the school premises so as to stop anybody leaving the school grounds. As soon as the siren sounds to end break, they immediately proceed to start whipping people into the classrooms. They do not even allow a reasonable time for people to get from the school yard to classes, but they sjambok them to hasten their route to the classroom . . . I have subsequently seen bruises and cuts by these actions on many of my students . . . Pupils are being unlawfully assaulted and abused in an arbitrary fashion without reason.

Cases of mass arrests of school children were reported. In one instance a whole school of 1200 Soweto school children were [sic] arrested apparently for having left the school ground at a time when the emergency restrictions did not allow. The Supreme Court secured their release. I personally had an experience of battling with other ministers to have detained children of a primary school with their

SOUTH AFRICA'S WAR AGAINST CHILDREN

teachers because they broke the curfew regulations released. (Abantwana Bazabala, Detainees' Parents' Support Committee Report pp. 68–70.)

As recently as the beginning of September 1987 I received an SOS memo from a small Orange Free State dorp (village) Petrus Steyn, indicating that the onslaught against school children is still going on. People from the area reported that on September 2nd school children from the Secondary school called a boycott of classes to protest against the detention of two activists and against corporal punishment by the principal. When teachers at the primary school nearby heard about the boycott they sent the children home as a safety measure. As the children went home, it is alleged that the police arrived and attacked them with sjamboks. An unknown number of them were arrested and some treated for serious injuries.

Besides being terrorised at school, on the streets and in their houses, many of the children were detained and tortured. During the 1985 State of Emergency, of the 11,500 people detained 2,000 were children under sixteen. During the 1986 State of Emergency of the 22,000 detainees, 8,800 were children under eighteen (most of them between the ages of thirteen and eighteen). Some of them were under the age of nine. On November 3rd, 1986 there were 407 children in detention.

A memorandum of the Detainees' Parents' Support Committee (DPSC) says that as at September 22nd, 1987 the numbers of children detained under the June 1987 State of Emergency (according to records entered thus far) were 180. One of these children had spent 485 days in detention; 112 are still in detention now (September, 1987).

This policy of arbitrary terror has extended right into the detention cells. In a survey of sixty-five child detainees analysed by the DPSC only ten children could be identified as having organisational links and leadership responsibilities. Sixty-four of the sixty-five reported that they had been assaulted.

215

Many detained children have stated that they have been terrorised and assaulted in detention until they have "confessed" to crimes they have not committed.

Even the courts have been used as a weapon to terrorise children; children who have themselves been victims of security violence are often charged for "public violence". If you have been shot, for instance, you are assumed to have been committing a crime. You are detained and brought to justice, as they would say! According to the Minister of Law and Order, over 1,100 people were charged with public violence in 1986 alone. What the minister's figures do not show, though, are the vast numbers of children who were convicted on false evidence and those who were acquitted or had their charges dropped for lack of evidence.

Occasionally the gross injustice of the whole process is exposed, as in the case in September of last year of the twelve-year-old boy who had charges of public violence dropped against him. The boy, a standard two pupil from Parys, had spent eleven months in detention under the emergency regulations. The State alleged that he had confessed to throwing stones at the car of a township superintendent in June 1986. But the defence lawyer discovered that the said "confession" had been written in Afrikaans, a language that the boy did not understand. Charges against him and three others were dropped. (New Nation, September 10th, 1987.)

The Goals of Repression

From the above analysis, it is clear that the strategy of using the state repressive apparatus is not a rare one. It is not as if apartheid South Africa was forced into this situation because of the unrest in the country. I believe that this strategy was built into the whole "total strategy". It was meant to silence and suppress those who refused to collaborate with the efforts of the system to maintain white domination in the country.

The goal of this strategy of repression, therefore, is to beat our people to submission and create a political wasteland to enable the state to continue with its reforms. In South Africa, one does not need to have been violent to face the brutal hand of this system. One needs only to differ with the system, or expose the intention of these reforms, detect that they are meant to retrench apartheid and retain power in the hands of the white racist minority to qualify for brutalisation by this system.

Today, Chris Ngcobo, Jabu Mtshali, Nkululeko Douglas Mhlobi, Sidima Kabanyane, Phila Ngqumba, Mxolisi Jackson Juzile, Raymond Sutner, Amos Masondo, and many other leaders of the UDF who have since been in detention under the State of Emergency regulations for well over a year without any charges preferred against them have not raised their hands or picked up a stone against anyone. What have Patrick Lekota, Popo Molefe, Moss Chikane and others in the Delmas Treason Trial done except be lamentably peaceful in their struggle to end apartheid in South Africa?

The members of the National Education Crisis Committee (NECC), Vusi Khanyile, Molefe Tsele, Mr Mogase, who are now languishing in prison: what have they done except negotiate reasonably with the government to try and resolve the education crisis? And what of Eric Molobi, who is the only remaining member of the NECC executive, and has had to be in hiding for almost a year now to avoid being detained by the apartheid security forces? Did the NECC not talk to Deputy Minister of Education, De Beer, then Deputy Minister of Police, Vlok and to others, to resolve the education crisis? The only reason I can see for their being hunted down is that they did not readily agree with the strategies of the regime and therefore had to be removed from the scene to leave only those black "faces" who would agree.

For this reason, I am convinced that the demand on the ANC to abandon violence before the regime can negotiate with it is just bluff. It is a smokescreen to avoid facing the reality of genuine negotiations which will interfere with the dominant position of whites in this country. I mean to argue that violence is not an issue but white power is the issue here.

I cannot but reject the proposed National Statutory Council because it can only come into existence after suppressing all democratic patriots of South Africa, leaving out the co-optable elements of the black community to participate. Anyway, the National Council can never be an effective negotiating organ, in the same way that the tri-cameral system cannot be, because it is part of the apartheid system, and ensures that racism is secure. If the state were genuine about negotiations it would unban the liberation movements, release Mandela and other political prisoners, and let those in exile come back home to participate in it.

The regime's strategy of counter-revolution, as articulated by Vlok, Malan and others, is first, to engage in generalised terror against our people, supposedly crushing revolutionaries and radicals, beating them to submission or removing them from the scene. Secondly, it wants to engage in limited economic and political reforms to pacify the people and try to win their "hearts and minds" and thirdly, to introduce the so-called new dispensation in a political vacuum to enable it to secure white power domination. This is the so-called three-phase strategy of counter-revolution.

I call upon the international community to come in in defence of the southern African states which are under attack by apartheid forces and agents.

I wish to take this opportunity to represent the views and feelings of the majority of the peace-loving South Africans by calling on the international community to put pressure on South Africa to force it to abandon the

SOUTH AFRICA'S WAR AGAINST CHILDREN

apartheid system and allow all the people of South Africa to set up a new government based on a new constitution to establish a united, just and non-racial, democratic South Africa.

Trade Unions and Development

CARL WRIGHT

Carl Wright is Assistant Director at the Commonwealth Secretariat, London. The One World article was written in his previous capacity as Director of the Commonwealth Trade Union Council (1980–7).

He had since 1973/4 had extensive contacts with trade unionists and Labour leaders throughout the world and has served on Commonwealth Expert Groups on New Technology (1984–5) and Youth Unemployment (1986–7) and as adviser to the UN Centre on Transnational Corporations (1978–80); he also assisted in the drafting of the Labour Party's Development Charter (1985–6).

Carl Wright was born in 1950 and grew up in West Wales; he studied at University College, London and Reading University (1968–72). He lives with his wife in West Hampstead, London and is a member of the Transport and General Workers' Union.

Introduction

In Britain and many developed countries trade unionism is under attack. Membership has shrunk and employers and governments are making the most of a weaker trade union movement. In developing countries unions often face a battle for survival and in South Africa or Latin America to be a trade union activist is courting death or torture. Despite this unions in the developing world are growing in strength; historically they are identified with the anti-colonial struggle and have shown considerable political and organisational resilience.

There are traditional ties between British unions and their counterparts overseas, especially in the former territories of the British empire – what is now the independent Commonwealth of Nations. Despite a different political and economic evolution, union structures and labour legislation show similarities, and a shared consciousness of independent trade unionism exists.

The British TUC has long assisted union development in the former colonies and is today taking a lead role on issues such as apartheid. However, it needs to bring many of its international policies and practices up to date. For example, the annual TUC Conference still has different categories of overseas visitors: fraternal delegates from America and Canada; invited guests from Europe and Japan; and a third category of essentially developing country trade unionists. The British trade union and Labour movement has much to contribute on account of its history and strength, but workers' solidarity has to be given real content in an age when frontiers have less meaning and employers are organised on a multinational basis.

Unions Overseas

Trade unionism in Africa has strong roots in the struggle for national independence. Even today the influence of unions in political life is often greater than the number of workers organised collectively would suggest. In country after country trade unions have been a vehicle for the voicing of political aspirations when legitimate political parties were banned by the colonial authorities. It was therefore in the trade union movement that political leaders such as Sikka Stevens of Sierra Leone, Tom Mboya of Kenya and Joshua Nkomo of Zimbabwe had their roots. It was also the trade unions – through industrial action and political agitation – which hastened the process of decolonisation.

The same phenomenon can today be seen in the freedom struggle in South Africa and Namibia. Following the banning of the South African Congress of Trade Unions (SACTU), and the repression of the 1970s, a new powerful trade union movement has developed despite the shackles of apartheid. The 1980s have seen a tremendous growth in black trade unions, particularly the National Union of Mineworkers, led by Cyril Ramaphosa. This development was consolidated with the establishment of the Congress of South African Trade Unions (COSATU) in 1985, and its identification with the African National Congress and adoption of the Freedom Charter as policy. The same process is now occurring in Namibia where the

National Union of Namibian Workers (NUNW) aligned to the South-West Africa People's Organisation (SWAPO), is at the centre of agitation for workers' rights. It is, therefore, not surprising that COSATU and NUNW have been singled out by the Pretoria regime for repression, being seen as the SACTU of the 1980s.

African unions were for many years divided by Cold War conflicts, resulting in competing national trade union centres, affiliated to different world labour organisations. In many ex-French colonies moreover, the rival French trade union structure found its local counterpart. The situation was particularly bad in Nigeria, the largest black African country, and led to the establishment of a strong, united Nigeria Labour Congress in 1978 with a strict policy of non-alignment. In other countries, too, single national centres were created, although sometimes at the direction of the Government with a view to exerting greater government control over workers.

Two major models of trade unions have developed – one where the unions are relatively free and autonomous, another where unions are a branch of the ruling party and virtually a government agency. Increasingly, however, more complex structures have evolved. In Tanzania the unions have taken an independent position from the CCM Party with which they are linked, whereas in Kenya, the Secretary General of the national trade union centre, generally considered autonomous, has to be endorsed upon election by the country's President. In other countries, such as Zimbabwe and the smaller frontline states, the trade union movement is still at a relatively early stage. The independently minded trade union movement of Zambia, centred on the copper belt mines, has had considerable differences with President Kaunda, who in turn has not hesitated to attack the union leadership.

Trade unions in black Africa – in Nigeria, in Ghana, in Zambia and elsewhere – have been at the heart of the campaign against the imposition of economic austerity measures dictated by the International Monetary Fund. Unions have not only defended the interests of their own membership and their families but the vast majority of the population in their countries who stand to suffer from IMF policies. It is, therefore, not surprising that unions are often seen at loggerheads with their governments, especially in one-party states, where they may represent an unofficial political opposition.

Union-Government conflicts and different models of trade unionism also exist in the Arab countries of North Africa and the Middle East. The often more rigid one-party or even feudal structures of these countries have, however, limited the development of strong independent trade unions in much of the Arab-Islamic world.

Caribbean workers have perhaps the most sophisticated trade unions in the developing world, born out of the independence struggle and dominated by major national political figures such as Manley and Bustamente. The rich diversity of West Indies political life is reflected in the trade union structures with many islands, even the smallest, having rival trade union organisations aligned to the competing political parties. In Jamaica, the National Workers' Union is linked to the socialist PNP while the Bustamente union is associated with the conservative JLP. Similar rivalries exist elsewhere. In Jamaica, a more hopeful development of late has been the establishment of a Joint Trade Union Research and Development Centre among the rival unions. Perhaps the most advanced organisation in the Caribbean is the Barbados Workers' Union, led by veteran trade union leader Frank Walcott, who has presided over rising living standards and social benefits for his members. The British TUC could learn from the BWU's PR programme which involves a syndicated column in the main Sunday newspaper and a regular slot on the national radio every week.

Despite their relative maturity, Caribbean trade unions still have many needs, which in some instances are influenced by the geopolitical environment. In many of the smaller East Caribbean islands, unions are fragmented and have low membership. Here basic trade union education is a priority. The trade union situation in Grenada following the 1983 US invasion has been turbulent, accentuated by external attempts to dominate it – including the arrival of US labour "experts" who appeared within days of the invasion. Belize is a special case, an oasis of peace and democracy in a strife-torn Central America; its small trade union movement, assisted by a Trade Union Institute sponsored by Canadian labour merits particular support.

The strong historical ties between Britain and the West Indies provide a basis for close Labour movement links. Today, when trade unionists of Caribbean origin such as the Assistant General Secretary of the TGWU are taking their rightful place in the British trade union movement, the case for cementing these ties is greater than ever.

Unions in South and Central America have suffered the vicissitudes of Latin American political life, and have at times faced most brutal and savage repression. Mexico has been something of an exception and its trade union movement, led by ninety-year-old veteran Fidel Velasquez has been a powerful, if conservative, institution. In Argentina, the main CGT trade union centre has traditionally had close links with Peronist populism. As in Africa, external influences have interfered in the name of either the Monroe Doctrine or world Communism. For these reasons it is imperative that British and European trade unionists take an active part in supporting democratic trade-union movements in Latin America, as they have been seeking to do in Nicaragua.

* * *

In Asia, apart from China, where trade unionism is beginning to develop a more distinct profile after years of isolation, the largest trade union movement exists in India. As elsewhere, Indian trade unions were closely associated with the struggle for national independence and the Textile Labour Association, centred in Ahmedabad, still proudly recalls its foundation by Gandhi in 1918.

India's trade unions grew alongside the political independence movement and already in the 1920s reached over 200,000 members, mostly organised in the All India TUC (AITUC). Today they number in the region of 10 million. While this is still a small proportion of the total work force Indian unions are reaching out to unorganised labour, especially in the countryside, by special union-run rural workers' programmes. A feature of Indian trade unions – like their Pakistani, Bangladeshi and Sri Lankan counterparts – is an excessive fragmentation along party political lines. The main national trade union centre – the Indian National TUC – is aligned to the ruling Congress Party, but there is a multitude of sizeable rival centres of socialist, Hindu-nationalist, or Communist tendency. This fragmentation has undoubtedly weakened the role of Asian trade unions, especially in countries like Pakistan where authoritarianism seeks to stifle free trade union activity. It also makes the task of British or other fraternal movements in rendering assistance more complex than if only one national trade union centre existed in each country.

The trade union situation in newly industrialised countries such as Singapore, Malaysia or South Korea varies considerably. In Singapore there is close identity between the Government of Lee Kuan Yew and the National TUC, reflected in the fact that the latter's General Secretary is also Deputy Prime Minister. In Malaysia a different model exists, complicated by the ethnic divisions of the country and the strength of trade unions among mainly

Indian-origin plantation workers. In South Korea, trade unions, like democratic parties, are still fighting for fundamental freedoms.

A special situation exists in the Philippines following the overthrow of the Marcos dictatorship. Here the KMU trade union is in the vanguard of workers' struggles and requires priority support from fraternal organisations. Mention should also be made of Indonesia – a country with one of the world's largest populations – where the military regime keeps official trade union activity on a tight rein.

Events in Fiji in 1987 focussed world attention on the Pacific. It is insufficiently understood that the military coup in Fiji deposed a democratically elected Labour Government established by the Fiji TUC and elected on a radical platform of wealth redistribution and support for a nuclear-free Pacific. Inter-communal tensions only developed later and obscured the non-racial nature of the Labour Government.

Apart from Fiji, trade unionism in the small Pacific islands is of very recent origin and still developing. In many of the islands, unions are active on the plantations, in the ports and in the public sector. In some countries – such as Tonga – unions are still struggling for recognition while in others – such as Kiribati – they experienced early confrontations with their governments. The Labour movements in Australia and New Zealand provide an obvious means of channelling support to these fledgling organisations and it is important that Great Power Politics in the Pacific does not interfere with their autonomous development.

Workers Divided

International trade unionism is as old as trade unionism itself: some hundred years ago workers in Europe were

229

organising cross-frontier contacts and planning joint actions. It is from this time that the earliest trade union internationals – the International Trade Secretariats, for example for miners, for transport workers, or metal workers – date. The cause of international workers' solidarity was dealt a savage blow by World War I – a war which many in the European Labour movement had believed would be prevented by that very same solidarity. The post-1917 schism between the Communist and the Socialist and Social Democratic movements created a deep division in the world Labour movement which still remains today.

A brief attempt to establish a united World Federation of Trade Unions (WFTU) took place in the immediate aftermath of World War II, but Cold War politics soon resulted in the creation of a western-orientated International Confederation of Free Trade Unions (ICFTU), leaving a rump WFTU dominated by Moscow. Another international is the small World Confederation of Labour, (WCL), with membership in a limited number of countries, in particular Latin America, influenced by the Catholic Church.

Post-1945 Cold War divisions mean that trade unions in developing countries have been a constant battleground for rival ideologies often quite alien to the needs of those countries and their workers. The 1970s saw a reaction against Cold War politics, leading to the establishment of regional bodies, such as the Organisation of African Trade Unity (OATUU), based on strict nonalignment, and the European Trade Union Confederation (ETUC), seeking to unite all trade unions in Western Europe. It was also a period when international trade unions were responding to the North-South problem and the challenge of multinational companies. In the International Labour Organisation (ILO), too, "East" and "West" unions were increasingly coming together in practical issues such as health and safety at work.

The renewed international tensions of the 1980s and the accompanying worldwide economic recession has meant a return – hopefully temporarily – to more rigid Cold War politics. In the case of the ICFTU, the re-affiliation of the American Federation of Labour and Congress of Industrial Organizations (AFL-CIO), which had isolated itself in the 1970s under George Meany, meant that the anti-Communist attitudes of US labour were given greater expression, to the dismay of the more detente-minded ICFTU affiliates. Anti-Communism has also been a preoccupation of the American "Free Labour Institutes", linked to the AFL-CIO and funded by the US State Department and their influence in the developing world has been substantial, having millions of dollars at their disposal.

An important development in the 1980s was the creation of the Commonwealth Trade Union Council, (CTUC), in 1978/1980. Originally viewed as of little significance with few resources, the CTUC soon developed into a real force in international trade unionism, bringing together trade unions from North and South and with membership across the ideological boundaries. It proved itself adept at using its limited means to maximum effect, concentrating support on unions with particular needs as in post-1980 Zimbabwe, Uganda after the fall of Amin, newly independent Pacific and Caribbean countries and, most importantly, South Africa and Namibia. The non-aligned nature of the CTUC and its ability to develop programmes of practical solidarity meant that it was regarded with unease in certain quarters with vested interests but seen as a breath of fresh air by unions in developing countries.

Trade unions in the developing world are unfortunately still subjected to external ideological manipulation, and individual corruption and financial mismanagement are sometimes a consequence. In Africa, in particular, the two superpowers have sought to cultivate a clientele, and in more than one country domestic union leadership elections have been influenced by external funds.

It is precisely for this reason that there has been a growing regionalisation of trade union activities and a demand for non-ideologically motivated assistance, particularly from the British TUC, the Canadian Labour Congress, Nordic trade unions and bodies such as the CTUC or ILO.

It is important that the British Labour movement plays a role appropriate to its status and membership, which is the second largest in the ICFTU and the largest in the CTUC and ETUC. The TUC has much in common with progressive unions, whether in Commonwealth countries, the Netherlands or Nordic countries and it must divorce itself from any remaining Cold War attitudes. Such an approach should, however, be consistent: it is ironical that the British National Union of Miners (NUM) aligned itself with the East Bloc miners' unions after the 1984/5 miners' strike when most solidarity during the strike came from Western countries, whereas Eastern European coal continued to be imported during the dispute.

Practical Solidarity

The British Trade Union Movement has much to contribute, not so much in history or traditions, which may be peculiar to the British Isles, but in modern responses to workers' education and in confronting the challenges of the 1980s – such as privatisation, new technology and union-busting. One of the great successes of the TUC and CTUC was to be among the first – together with the Nordic trade unions – in applying study circle and student-centred learning methods, avoiding formal lectures.

These methods minimise the "big brother" approach and provide an effective way of encouraging internal union democracy at a time when many unions still have hierarchical structures. It was significant that the Congress of South African Trade Unions, which adopted strict non-aligned policy following its inaugural Congress in 1985, looked to the TUC and CTUC for educational assistance, although incredibly this was almost blocked by an unreasonable insistence that all aid should exclusively be channelled through the ICFTU.

Central to achieving practical solidarity is a broad-based understanding of international trade unionism. Knowledge should not be restricted to members of the Head of the TUC International Department: it is essential that union officers and officials at shop steward level are given the opportunity to obtain first-level knowledge about international issues. The rank-and-file membership, too, must be provided with information, if workers' solidarity is to have any real meaning.

Trade union education is at the heart of ensuring that international trade union policy is not seen as an abstract, specialist area. International issues should be demonstrated as being of direct concern to individual trade unionists and their living and working conditions. One way of doing this is to draw the link between workers in Britain and their overseas counterparts who work for the same multinational company – often on appalling wages and in bad working conditions. Another way is to focus on specific issues, such as apartheid, where common links may exist through British employers.

Unions such as the TGWU or the NUM have long-standing ties with their counterpart unions overseas, although usually these have tended to be in developed countries, especially Europe and North America. This is, however, now changing and links are being forged further afield. Some unions, such as the National and Local Government Officers' Association (NALGO), have special international schools where wider issues are discussed. The TUREG group at Ruskin College took an early role in developing educational materials on trade unions and development and since the mid-1980s the CTUC and TUC have had a joint programme of development education for British trade unionists. The latter programme seeks to utilise the extensive TUC, trade union and Workers' Educational Association (WEA) educational network to raise international issues; already a series of regional TUC workshops have been held and a range of educational "packs" have been written. The next step must be to hold activities at local and individual union level, and to integrate international issues into regular trade union education, including the TUC's "Open School" programme of distance learning.

The One World organisation chaired by Glenys Kinnock can play a key role in raising awareness of international issues in the wider Labour movement. A trade union support group for One World has been established, intended to target union audiences and to develop materials of particular interest to trade unionists. In addition, One World is holding regional conferences throughout Britain with special workshops for trade unionists.

Once greater awareness has been achieved – Labour Aid must take on the same dimension as Bob Geldof's Live Aid – solidarity will develop naturally. There is, of course, already much existing solidarity through union-to-union links, individual initiatives and appeals and ad hoc contacts. In addition, solidarity is rendered through the international trade union movement – the International Trade Secretariats, the ICFTU and, increasingly, the CTUC. All this work, however, suffers from a certain lack of priority – domestic policy matters predominate and international issues are of secondary importance.

Existing solidarity work also suffers from lack of

resources. In many countries, especially the Nordic countries, government aid agencies allocate literally millions of pounds each year to national trade union centres for international solidarity work. Under the last Labour Government, the TUC received a modest Overseas Development Administration grant for this work, but this was slashed under the Thatcher Government, as were public funds for scholarships and study visits for overseas trade unionists. In recent years the TUC, working with the CTUC, has been able to restore some of the resources for international solidarity work. It has also tried to launch its own Union Aid charity. Overall resources are, however, still minimal, even compared to those being channelled through progressive charities such as War on Want. While there is some sign of change in ODA attitudes, substantial ODA funding for international trade union work will have to await the return of a Labour Government. For these reasons it is all the more important that greater awareness of the need for international solidarity is achieved through grass root education programmes and through the activities of One World.

In the meantime, much can nonetheless be done even with limited funds. Trade union officials can be seconded to work on overseas trade union projects. Union colleges and schools, as well as local education authority facilities, can be used to accommodate developing country trade unionists on study visits or short-term attachments. Specific projects or appeals can be supported, for example for women trade unionists who have been neglected: the first-ever visit of African women trade unionists to Britain took place in 1986! Attempts should also be made to facilitate exchange visits and "twinnings" with union branches overseas: this could be particularly valuable at shop steward level and it is regrettable that overseas contacts are often guarded jealously by professional trade union bureaucrats.

Conclusion

Trade unions in the developing world are alive and well – in fact, they often show an innovative spirit and a dynamism that some of their developed country brothers and sisters could well emulate.

Developing country unions are frequently in the vanguard of political and social struggles – whether for national liberation, as in South Africa, or in marshalling mass opposition to IMF austerity programmes. It is nonsense to view them as of minor importance or limited to defending the interests of an employed urban minority – beliefs beloved of some development economists whose experience is often confined to a small professional élite, with little contact with ordinary men or women in their own countries, let alone in the developing world.

Trade unions everywhere have a responsibility to develop closer links and to make common cause. In the age of multinational capital and inter-governmental decision-making, workers' solidarity across frontiers still lags far behind. The growing realisation of similar aspirations and common challenges, as well as problems, will make for stronger workers' solidarity. The ever-greater possibilities for modern communications will assist this trend: Workers of the World Unite will become less of a slogan and more of a reality as the 1980s give way to the 1990s.

Foreign Debt for One World

HUGH O'SHAUGHNESSY

Hugh O'Shaughnessy is the Latin American Correspondent of the *Observer* and has been writing about the region for more than twenty-five years. He was in Grenada during the US invasion of that island in 1983 and subsequently wrote *Grenada: Revolution, Invasion and Aftermath*. He is a frequent broadcaster, and his book, *Latin Americans*, accompanied a BBC Radio 4 series of the same name in 1988.

He received a British Press Award in 1984 and prizes from Columbia University and the University of Arkansas in the United States. He is a member of the Fabian Society, and has written and contributed to various Fabian pamphlets. He was first Chairman of the Latin American Bureau and is Vice-Chairman of the Executive Committee of IRELA (Institute for European-Latin American Relations).

The cause of One World may yet be helped by the debt crisis.

The idea may seem novel, even far-fetched, but after nearly a decade of trench warfare, of quarrelling, backbiting and brinkmanship between moneylenders in the rich countries and borrowers in the Third World, the contenders know that the time has come for some sort of armistice. The armies of politicians, bankers and diplomats on each side have done battle and have fought each other to a standstill. There is no alternative but to come to agree that in the matter of finance, as in many other matters, there is only one world.

The history of the debt crisis can be told briefly. The Arab-Israeli war of 1973 allowed the oil producers, mainly grouped in the Organization of Petroleum Exporting Countries, to raise massively the price of their products. Many of the most important of those producers were countries with tiny populations. After they had spent all the money they could have prudently disposed of – and often a lot more besides – they still had billions of dollars left. The OPEC surplus rose from $7,000 million in 1973 to $68,000 million the following year.

These surpluses the oil producers put into the banks of the rich countries where they expected it at least to earn interest. Money lodged in banks does not create interest by magic. The bankers had to lend the money on to borrowers and borrowers were not long in presenting themselves. Many Third World countries, particularly those who had no oil of their own and who could scarcely afford to pay the new high prices for the imported oil on which they had come to rely, were first in the queue. But such was the glut of money which poured into the Western banks from the oil producers that before long the representatives of those banks were queueing at the doors of potential lenders in the Third World pressing money on them. Much of this lending was unwise. The lenders went on lending even when it was becoming clear that the borrowers had borrowed too much. They went on lending even when they knew that borrowers were using money they had obtained for one scheme to finance something completely different. Western governments, seeing that "the petro-dollars were being re-cycled", left the increasingly powerful internationalised and autonomous financial markets to themselves. Unwilling or unable to control them day by day, they were equally unwilling to indulge in long-term financial strategies.

From 1979 onwards the situation got worse as the fight against what was seen as excessive inflation in the western world was fought with "monetarist" policies and a sharp rise in world interest rates. It was soon to be shown that the poorer countries with a lot of borrowings were not able to pay these higher interest rates. In August 1982 the Government of Mexico announced that it could not meet its debts. The world debt crisis was under way with a vengeance.

With hindsight it is easy to see that a great deal of irresponsibility was being indulged in. That same hindsight shows that the irresponsibility was shared by borrowers and lenders alike. But as the threat to the world financial system developed it was not the time for judicious apportioning of blame and statesmanlike international compromises. Everyone ran for cover. Among those who ran fastest were the Western governments who tried to establish the principle that the debt crisis was a matter for the commercial banks.

The Western banks and governments both in fact saw that the whole financial structure of the world would be in jeopardy if in any concerted way the debtors joined up to repudiate their commitments. Throughout the middle years of this decade therefore, Western banks and governments followed a strategy of promoting deals under which the debtor governments were obliged to pay the maximum possible proportion of their incomes on debt servicing. They were told to cut their imports and maximise their exports in order to save and earn the hard currency needed to repay the bankers. Very importantly, the Western governments and banks, themselves well interlinked in such organisations as the Organisation for Economic Co-operation and Development, made sure that their debtors did not achieve a similar degree of co-ordination. The creditors managed to minimise the effect on their negotiating positions of the divisions which existed between the US and the British banks who had put comparatively little aside in the form of provisions against bad debts and the bankers of Continental Europe whose provisions were higher.

The creditors also insisted that concessions on debt servicing obligations could be given to the debtor countries only on an individual "case by case" basis. For their part, each debtor was keen to promote its individual interests with the groups of bankers it faced by arguing that its case was special.

The debtors paid heavily for their lack of commitment to co-operation with each other. The united creditors were able to pick off, negotiate and, in many cases, impose terms on the divided debtors, often allowing them longer to pay but charging them fully for the privilege. In the interests of servicing their debt the governments of the debtor countries cut their imports drastically and did what they could – which often was not much given the wave of protectionism which was sweeping the industrialised world – to increase exports. The crisis hitting the Third World was seen as a temporary affair which they could overcome if they were willing to show moral fibre.

They were urged by bodies like the International Monetary Fund to cut government expenditure. This process certainly helped to put an end to some wasteful expenditures which had been afforded during the times of easy money but it almost always also reduced the standard of living of the poorest who were most dependent on the services such as education and health which the state was aiming to provide. The burden was rarely carried by those who could best afford it in the debtor countries and unemployment grew and grew.

The effort was not sufficient because the task was excessively hard. Several South American countries in the mid-1980s were due to pay out to foreign creditors sums far greater than their total earnings from exports. In 1983, for instance, Argentina was due to pay 149.4 per cent of its export earnings and Bolivia, a far poorer country which stopped servicing its debt entirely, had to pay a similar proportion. There were several rallying calls from among the ranks of the debtors. When he was sworn in as President of Peru in July 1985 Latin America's youngest leader Alan Garcia said that his country would pay no more than ten per cent of what the country earned for its exports to service its debt and called on other debtors to follow the Peruvian lead. The Latin Americans did not follow. Nor did they respond when President Fidel Castro called for a concerted reneging on the foreign debt by the Third World.

The policy of mending and patching and leaving the initiatives principally to the commercial bank creditors in the industrialised world that was the outcome of the creditors' eagerness for repayment and the debtors' inability to agree on concerted action was seen to be inadequate as early as October 1985.

(In the years which followed the outbreak of the debt

crisis one curious circumstance was the forcefulness with which the banking lobby in the rich countries presented its case. It contrasted oddly with the relative silence of the industrialists and exporters whose markets in the Third World were being taken away as the poorer countries were universally urged to import less. While the bankers appeared to have the ear of their governments in pressing on them the case for making the Third World reduce its growth rates, the industrialists seemed mute as the orders they were used to receiving from the poorer countries fell away and added to the difficulties they were suffering in their domestic markets. US exports to Latin America fell by a quarter between 1981 and 1985, total imports by Latin America and the Caribbean dropped by 40 per cent and Claude Cheysson, the European Community Commissioner, said that the fall off in orders from the Third World could have cost perhaps 3,000,000 jobs in Europe.)

In October 1985 the then Secretary to the US Treasury, James Baker, announced a plan under which official lending institutions would join the commercial banks in making new money available to the major debtors. The Baker scheme called for fifteen of the largest debtors to become the beneficiaries of $29 billion of extra financing, $9 billion of which would come from the international financial institutions such as the World Bank, the balance coming from new lending from the commercial banks. In return the debtors were expected to change their economic strategies to give more importance to market forces and the private sector. The $29 billion was clearly inadequate when the combined debt of the fifteen selected beneficiaries by that time was well over $430 billion. Nor did the Baker plan do anything for many smaller debtors who were often in worse straits than the bigger ones.

The Baker Plan was not adequate. In February 1987 Brazil announced that it was suspending indefinitely the servicing of more than $80,000 million of its total debt of around $110,000 million. During most of the 1980s Brazil had increased exports remarkably and had restricted imports but by 1986 that was no longer possible as Brazil's spectacular growth in exports was being choked off.

Since the clear failure of the Baker Plan to shore up the existing system the realisation that the present situation is unsustainable has begun to be shared by the creditors as well as the debtors.

In May 1987 Citicorp, a New York bank, once a hardliner in trying to keep the creditors to their agreement, publicly acknowledged that it would be unlikely to get much of its money back. It raised the amount of the reserves it had put aside to meet bad debts from less than five per cent to around a quarter of its Third World loans. The action punctured the principle hitherto sustained that whoever was to lose money and make sacrifices it would not be the banks. It was an example which had to be followed by its US and British competitors even though this meant the banks announced losses. (Continental European banks had already made large provisions in a more discreet form.)

A further principle was punctured at the end of 1987 when J. P. Morgan, another New York bank, collaborated with the US Treasury in a financial scheme for Mexico. Under the scheme commercial banks were offered US-backed 20-year bonds in exchange for the debt due for more immediate payment. The importance of this scheme was that it involved the banks selling their rights to payment in the short term at a great discount for the sake of better security in the long term. The scheme recognised what had been the case for several years, namely that bankers holding documents which theoretically assured them of payment from governments who could not in fact pay, could and did sell those documents to others at a big discount.

A third principle was punctured in the case of the

Mexican deal, that of Third World debt to commercial banks being looked at by governments as merely a question for the commercial banks themselves. Anxious at the prospect of political tension rising in Mexico, the US Government, through its Treasury, became involved, issuing its guarantee to promote a scheme which would lighten the debt burden on an important neighbour.

For its part the British Government, which had usually aligned its financial strategies with those of the US Government, took the lead in lightening the burden of some countries in the matter of their repaying British government development loans. Several billion dollars-worth of British Government loans in hard currencies were converted into debts in local currency or written off entirely. The West German Government has been cancelling its claims on the poorer countries.

Governments in the richer countries are realising that the debt crisis is too important a phenomenon to be left in the hands of commercial bankers.

The debtor countries, who at the beginning of the decade were arguing this very point unavailingly to the creditors, are finding a new receptiveness to their arguments now that they have demonstrated through their various moratoriums that the fortunes of the commercial banks of the richer countries are indeed in jeopardy.

The change of mood was well expressed in the All Party Parliamentary Group on Overseas Development which in a report published in 1987 declared,

"Debt has ceased to be a purely banking problem and now requires a political solution. With firm political will, the British Government could again lead an international initiative to give debt relief . . .

"The issue must be treated at the level of governments. All interested parties, debtors as well as creditors, developed and developing countries must be heard. All the issues, economic and social as well as financial, must be covered. That is why we believe the United Nations to be the most appropriate forum. We propose therefore that the UK Government now take the debt issue to the United Nations General Assembly. We believe that support should be urgently sought for the spirit of our recommendations from the Commonwealth, our European partners, the United States and Japan."

In this context one of the blocks to action by Britain which could be effective in relieving Third World debt is that the possibility for joint action within the European Community on financial matters is limited. Britain has not even accepted the case for participation in the exchange rate mechanism of the European Monetary system, a vital first step towards co-ordinating Europe's financial strength in the way that the Community's trading strength is already mustered. Sooner or later that step must be taken. The vision of One World cannot credibly be preached by those who baulk at the idea of One Region and who reject greater co-ordination with their immediate neighbours.

The support which exists in Britain for a political solution to the debt crisis and which will be turned into action by the next Labour government must be part of a European – or at least European Community – strategy. The suggestion has been made in a paper produced by the institute for European-Latin American Relations that the Community should create a Community Foreign Debt Committee with representatives of the Commission, government ministries and central banks. It could be a useful initiative in formulating specific proposals from Europe in this area. If Third World debt is too important an issue to be left to bankers, it is also too big a subject to be tackled by one government, however wellmeaning.

Nicaragua's Need for International Co-operation

MIGUEL D'ESCOTO

Born in 1933, Miguel d'Escoto was educated in the United States where he received degrees in theology and education. He was ordained a priest in 1962 and in the following year went to Chile where he worked in Santiago with the inner-city poor until 1969. There he founded the National Institute of Population Action and Social Research with a view to improving the living conditions of the poor. It was with this aim in mind that he made trips to Brazil and Mexico to evaluate pastoral work in the "misery zones" there. In 1979, back in Nicaragua, he continued this work by founding the Nicaraguan Foundation for Integral Community Development.

From 1975 onwards, Father Miguel d'Escoto became increasingly involved with the anti-Somozist struggle, and in October 1977 joined the Group of Twelve – fellow scholars and professionals committed to ending Somoza's rule. With the triumph of the Revolution in July 1979, Father Miguel d'Escoto was named Foreign Minister. Since September 1980 he has also been a member of the Sandinista Assembly.

The aims and aspirations of nearly every sector of the population were brought together in the Nicaraguan Revolution. There was, perhaps, nothing quite like it in the world. It could only compare with some of the African revolutions where black majorities have taken power from European oligarchies.

Workers, peasants, businessmen and the international community joined forces: they isolated Somoza, brought down his tyranny and then, with the new Government, became the creators and members of the new economy, a mixed economy. Recognition of the part the international community could play in the new economy was formally stated in the first national economic plan – The 1980 Plan. This explicitly stated:

> The programme of recovery must first stimulate awareness of the size of the problems and the tremendous difficulties and limitations that confront the Revolution. These must be overcome before we can escape from the crisis created by the Somoza dictatorship, in which the country has suffered from a scarcity of institutional, economic and human resources.
>
> The people, the Government, private enterprise and the international community must be made aware of this critical situation so that the efforts of Nicaraguans and the international community, working together for a single purpose, will enable a rapid recovery to be made without prolonging or increasing the sufferings of our people.

The reference to the international community as a participant in the new economy was set out in The 1980 Plan
as follows:

> The international community would facilitate recov-
> ery by giving full co-operation, providing technical
> support, and showing a sense of responsibility for our
> country's plight, by flexible restructuring of our for-
> eign debt and showing courteous consideration for
> the past experience of our people.

As can be seen the Sandinista political and economic
Plan was marked from the first by its commitment to the
international community, which was included as an
integral part of the Revolution. At the same time it is
expected that this commitment will be matched by an
international respect for the good intentions of the Plan
and an understanding to help us surmount our difficulties
by providing financial and technical co-operation.

Uncompromising Non-Alignment

The economic plan put forward faced up to Nicaragua's
previous role in international affairs. It expressed shame
because the Somoza Government had provided a platform
for the United States invasions of fellow Latin American
countries, and had not taken its own position in international affairs but had assumed one imposed by the United
States. Only by correcting this attitude could national
dignity be regained.

In consequence, diplomatic relations were opened with
many different countries, whatever their political, economic and social regimes. Nicaragua became an active
member of the Non-Aligned Movement; relations with
the rest of Latin America were broadened; and the right
to establish relations with Socialist countries was
restored. At the same time, and in spite of the Reagan
Administration's efforts to divide Central America, the

Nicaraguan Government maintained an active dialogue with its neighbours. This policy made the Esquipulas Accord possible, and enabled foundations to be laid on which regional peace could be built.

Since July 1979, Nicaragua's own views have been heard in UNCTAD, GATT, SELA and the General Assembly of the United Nations. And, together with its neighbours, Nicaragua has been an active and respected participant in delegations to the European Economic Community.

The Structure of Underdevelopment, the Need for Reconstruction, and the Devastation Caused by Aggression

At the time of the revolutionary triumph, in its economic structure and status within the international system, Nicaragua displayed the typical devastation of a dependent, underdeveloped capitalist state. Commerce depended on a few agricultural crops grown for export, and an unstable foreign exchange income produced by these exports became the main source of funding for imports.

In the face of Nicaragua's limited – or rather, devastated – industrial development, the economy was forced to purchase equipment, machinery, means of transport and other essentials from abroad.

Industry, built up during the sixties as part of the scheme of Central American integration, did not facilitate the production of capital goods, but rather of consumer goods. In addition, industry had not been developed: it used obsolete machinery from the United States which made it very dependent on imported spares and replacements.

The dependence on imported technology for agriculture and industry was intensified by a dependence on imported sources of energy.

251

The Revolution sought to change this dependence and also to put an end to the Somoza family's selfish exploitation of its economic power. The inequitable system of land ownership and expenditure of national income, and the continuation of very low standards in education and health clashed violently and shockingly with the luxury enjoyed by this dominant family with its swollen deposit accounts in Miami.

However, the attempt to alter this structure of under-development and inequality met its first great obstacle in the high cost of the struggle against Somoza. According to well-known international agencies like CEPAL, the costs of physical destruction, the loss of capital stolen by the Somozists, wasted funds and the great burden of foreign debt inherited from the Somoza regime, amount to thousands of millions of dollars.

Hopes of travelling the path of development, of building a democratic society in which the centres of decision-making would be brought back to Nicaragua from abroad, were faced with thousands of impediments.

The first two years of the new revolutionary Government showed the potential of a mixed economy working in the service of the people. Before the aggression against Nicaragua began, production during 1980 and 1981 showed a significant rate of growth, and the fruits of that growth were shown in the multiplying of health services, the building of homes and reduction of illiteracy. While the rate of growth was higher than the average for Latin America, the rate of investment reached even greater heights, and was to be used to provide a solid foundation for the future of Nicaraguan society.

In those two years, from a position where there had long been an urgent need for reconstruction and change, we succeeded in coming to grips with the limitations that the Revolution faced at the time of its triumph. Our aims were realised through the passion of the whole nation for building a new society, and we attracted solid support from the international community.

As has been adequately demonstrated in *Aid That Counts*, The Hague 1988, by Solon Barraclough and others, edited by the Transnational Institute in collaboration with CRIES, foreign aid has played a crucial role in Nicaragua:

> The new Nicaragua was able to accommodate many different forms of development assistance from a variety of donors. Aid in the form of emergency relief was used for reconstruction after the Revolution and for the victims of the 1982 floods and the Contra War. The Government's large-scale investment projects attracted concessionary loans to support economic growth. Other aid designed to improve the living standards of the poor went to both governmental and community programmes in health, education, housing, welfare, and the provision of drinking water. Numerous initiatives emphasising popular participation drew aid for self-help development and the organisation of the poor.
>
> Some donor governments and agencies sought to use development assistance as a political lever to constrain the overtly non-aligned stance of the new Government. Other, more commercially motivated, sources provided aid and concessionary credit as a means of creating or expanding their markets in the region. The Nicaraguan Government did not, however, accept offers of "assistance" accompanied by conditions that contradicted the development of principles and objectives it had laid down.

Political and economic support for an alternative way of development was expressed not only by progressive governments and countries, but also by moderate ones in Latin America, Europe and the Third World.

Unfortunately, however, the United States Government headed by Ronald Reagan began to use a strategy for overthrowing the Sandinista Government that had been devised at Santa Fe. It spurned the Nicaraguan people's longing for reconstruction and reform, and deliberately ignored the international community's more positive attitude of collaboration with the Sandinistas.

During barely two years of respite, macroeconomic growth and balance were achieved. Then, as soon as the Reagan Administration's offensive started, it began to damage the Nicaraguan economy. It distorted the economy, putting a brake on development so that growth became hard to maintain. This has caused further suffering for the people of Nicaragua.

The Reagan Administration's assault upon our economy has had these effects:

1. By using mercenaries to wage war, it has caused damage costing US$3.8 billion in loss of production and harm to the infrastructure, through capital lying idle and disturbance of social services. Besides this, there is the incalculable loss through the tragic deaths of a multitude of innocent men, women and children.

2. The embargo upon commercial and financial dealings between Nicaragua and her traditional markets in the United States cost Nicaragua more than US$600 million in lost trade. The door was closed against the purchase of spare parts and supplies – closed against a country of limited technology which had been totally dependent upon the United States.

3. The increasing cost of defence accounts for the whole of the fiscal deficit in the Government's budget. This has been the main cause of the inflation that the country has suffered since 1984. The standard of living for the Nicaraguan household has been lowered as much by inflation as

by the efforts of the Government to reduce the
fiscal deficit.

Peace and Central America

Added to all the costs imposed by the military, economic
and diplomatic aggression against Nicaragua itself, is the
economic deterioration of the whole Central American
region. This has affected Nicaragua directly and has
drastically reduced trade with neighbouring countries.

The United States' intention to isolate Nicaragua from
its neighbours has not been fulfilled, but commercial
relations have been affected. The militarisation of Hon-
duras and El Salvador, the creation of the Caribbean Basin
Initiative, and the attempts to destroy the Central American Common Market, have caused a serious regional
crisis which has created financial uncertainty and caused
people to invest elsewhere.

The regional crisis, aggravated by the United States
intervention, also derives from the enormous difficulties
brought about by an unfavourable international situation.
Foreign debt and a fall in the prices of basic export
commodities have made foreign exchange scarce and are
strangling the whole region. The present economic crisis
in the region is as serious for us as the world crisis of the
thirties Depression.

Peace for Central America is vital, both to end the
suffering and to enable us to resume development.

National, Regional and International Efforts to
Overcome the Crisis

On its own, Nicaragua cannot alter the basic causes of
underdevelopment in the region, find useful parts to play
in the international economic community, nor secure
the recovery of financial or commercial links in Central
America. Neither can it overcome its own economic

crisis alone. Nicaragua has already made efforts to attain these ends and willingly continues to do so.

The efforts made by the Government and people of Nicaragua to withstand the commercial embargo, to sustain Central American integration, and to overcome underdevelopment, have been unceasing since the Revolution began. However, the actions of the huge forces of imperial power and the unwillingess of powers allied to the United States to prevent or limit them have created an acute economic crisis in Nicaragua. In February 1988, the Nicaraguan Government, by an extraordinary mobilisation of all its resources, carried out a monetary reform and implemented a series of complementary measures designed to reduce inflation and the distortions of the pricing system. The reform, with its complementary measures, aims ultimately to increase production, decrease the foreign debt, and augment Nicaragua's economic potential which is being held back by the huge costs of defence already mentioned.

In parallel with these efforts, initiatives for peace have begun in Esquipulas. The proposals made included an agreement with the counter-revolutionaries for a cease-fire, and are essential to the success of the new economic measures. The Government is fully determined to strive for this success with all the resolve it can muster.

However, the international community must realise that the human and material losses sustained by Nicaragua ought not to be borne by her alone. There is an international responsibility for what happens to Nicaragua when the United States Government is in contempt of the International Court of Justice at the Hague.

At the same time, the Central American Common Market must recover the dynamism it once had. The fall in the value of trade within the region from US$1,200 million in 1980 to only US$370 million in 1987 affects not only Nicaragua, but every country of the region.

Therefore, Nicaragua's requests for international co-operation are as follows:

1. International funding to recover productive capacity, provide for food needs, and restore export activity.

   Adjustments made by the Nicaraguan Government in its domestic economy include cut-backs in the state sector to reduce public spending and set a more precise course for economic policy. These adjustments need to be complemented by the supply of hard currency and food donations which would provide additional resources for regulating the price of basic foods. Foreign exchange is also needed to give greater flexibility in the purchase of imported necessities, and, in the short term, to remove the strains caused by the necessity of devoting too much of available finance to imported goods.

2. Other countries and international banking must co-operate by removing the conditions set on the repayment of the old debt contracted by the Somoza regime. This is logical in that repayment has been made more difficult by the war in which the counter-revolutionaries have attacked productive projects as well as the infrastructure.

3. Technical and financial support for the recovery of Central American industry and trade, which would permit the development of industrial capacity in Central America as a whole, and in Nicaragua in particular.

   With this, it would be possible to restore trade between neighbouring countries to 1980 levels, and re-establish a system of payments between the countries of the region. This would have very important political repercussions on regional peace initiatives.

4. Assistance from European and other countries in investment and technology, with the aim of defining and implementing a new strategy for industrial development to make the best use of Nicaragua's resources; a proper integration of agriculture and industry; the use of technologies appropriate to local conditions so as to attract an effective work force; the substitution of imports.

5. Assistance in supplying the country's energy needs in the short term; a willingess to invest in the development of local sources of energy with the aim of decreasing national dependence and guaranteeing energy security in the medium term.

6. Assistance for increasing traditional exports which will continue, in the medium term, to be the main source of foreign-exchange income for Nicaragua and for the whole of Central America. This should be carried out by pre-financing harvests to ensure adequate levels of imports and maximum rate of production. But, in addition, it is essential that there should be free trade with Western Europe, so that we can export our products.

    Increasing protectionism and subsidies by the European Economic Community and other developed countries has tended to lower the prices of our exports. Therefore, effective assistance for Nicaragua and Central America means a commitment to eradicating such protectionist practices. At the same time, commitments should be made to regulate prices and so reduce the damaging fluctuations they suffer in the international market.

7. The continuation of support from non-governmental organizations (NGOs) for social development and grassroots communities, with the aim of improving standards of health, education and housing for the poor.

The Nicaraguan Government is clear about the need for international co-operation to overcome its state of under-development and to undertake the task of reconstruction that the war of aggression has imposed on it. There is no alternative: massive and decisive international co-operation is needed to help overcome the difficulties that the people of Nicaragua face. However, aid without conditions, respect for national sovereignty and self-determination are firm principles which must govern such collaboration. This is the understanding of the Nicaraguan Government which is asserted by the continuing national struggle against foreign aggression.

Index